BusinessWeek

MARKETING
Power Plays

BusinessWeek

MARKETING
P o w e r   P l a y s

How the World's Most

Ingenious Marketers

Reach the Top of Their Game

M c G r a w – H i l l
New York · Chicago · San Francisco
Lisbon · London · Madrid · Mexico City · Milan
New Delhi · San Juan · Seoul · Singapore
Sydney · Toronto

INTRODUCTION

From conversations we have every day with serious businesspeople like you, we know that you have an enormous need for news, information, and insight that is so accurate, reliable, and unbiased that you can act on it. That is what *BusinessWeek* is known for, and what we are always striving to do better.

Our *BusinessWeek* Power Plays series takes this to the next level. In collaboration with McGraw-Hill Professional books, we have drawn from the best in the business—the world's leading managers, strategists, and marketers—to analyze how you can use the best practices and best ideas of these insiders in your own personal playbook. Each chapter is drawn from a *BusinessWeek* case study and is supplemented with lesson plans to articulate the key learnings in each case study, "power moves" (practical tactics you can adapt to your own situations), and "Monday Morning" strategies to help you stay focused on success and put best practices into action. Plus a downloadable slide show and other online features available to readers from BusinessWeek.com/powerplays that will enable you to share these lessons with colleagues and team members, as well as brainstorm new ideas and strategies.

Each of our marketing case studies has been selected to illustrate how business models are being reinvented by global companies in industry segments from manufacturing to finance, from information technology to services. To refill the bucket in Caterpillar's extraordinarily cyclical "yellow iron" earthmoving equipment and heavy-duty engine business, for example, Chief Executive James W. Owens's power play is in financial services, logistics, and remanufacturing. Citigroup's Steven Freiberg, head of the newly carved out retail banking services group for the United States and Canada, must focus on organic growth to boost global Citi's also-ran domestic market.

Electrolux Chief Hans Straberg has tapped some 160,000 customers from around the globe to dream up its next batch of hot products. Marissa Mayer, Google's vice president for search products and user experience, leads the company's evaluation of new features for the search giant. Dr. Harlan Weisman, chief science and technology officer for Johnson & Johnson's device and diagnostic unit, is charged with identifying key new markets for devices as the 120-year-old company confronts the convergence of devices, drugs, and diagnostics. At Hewlett-Packard, the long-underachieving corporate computing business has been transformed by technology solutions group head Anne Livermore's laser focus on 15 key weaknesses.

Intel CEO Paul Otellini's power play is to blow up the brand and take the company into uncharted territory, such as consumer electronics, wireless communications, and health care. At General Electric, Jeffrey Immelt is turning the culture upside down, demanding far more risk and innovation. Germany's Albrecht brothers, Karl and Theo, who run the ultra-discount retailer Aldi and its U.S. sibling Trader Joe's, respectively, are seemingly unstoppable. IKEA's Ingvar Kamprad has built a global cult brand—and plans to keep it that way.

At 3M, James McNerney, an outsider, revitalized the company, Six Sigma-style; now, at Boeing, he is rebuilding the scandal-plagued aerospace giant. And no book on marketing power plays would be complete without Steve Jobs, who breathed new life into Apple, made Pixar into a movie powerhouse, and is now shaking up the world of entertainment as a Disney board member (and its largest shareholder).

This volume, *Marketing Power Plays*, also features material that provides readers with a broad look at major trends, demographic and cultural, that are altering the media and advertising landscape. Consumers are defining themselves in ever-narrower ways. Instead of aspiring to use the same brands as their neighbors, they search out unique products that represent them in a more personal way. But how do you reach these smaller and smaller niche audiences—or an audience of one? And even if you've figured it out, how do you keep your rivals from emulating your success? At ESPN, for example, boss George Bodenheimer's power play is to penetrate even more deeply into the lives of sports fans. At MTV, Chairman Judy McGrath must remake her TV empire fast enough to thrive in the Age of iPod. And Russell Simmons must bring his hip-hop empire and Phat Farm into the mainstream.

One note about these case studies: these chapters are drawn from up-to-the-minute *BusinessWeek* reporting and are therefore "snapshots in time." Every effort has been made to provide factual updates, but because of the nature of news reporting, some of the characters and circumstances that the stories are based upon have changed since the articles were originally written. We believe that the power plays in each case do stand the test of time and will provide valuable lessons, even in hindsight.

But the lessons from these individuals are just the building blocks for your own personal power plays—ideas that you will be able to put into use on Monday morning.

*　*　*

At *BusinessWeek*, many people have contributed the ideas and case studies in this book, including Tom Lowry, Mark Hyman, Ronald Grover, Roger Crockett, Michael Arndt, Mara Der Hovanesian, Cliff Edwards, Ariane Sains, Stanley Reed, Jack Ewing, Andrea Zammert, Wendy Zellner, Rachel Tiplady, Ellen Groves, Michael Eidam, Larry Armstrong, Peter Burrows, Amy Barrett, Kerry Capell, Cristina Lindblad, Ann Therese Palmer, Jason Bush, Dexter T. Roberts, Kenji Hall, Diane Brady, Ben Elgin, Heather Green, and Diane Alford. Special thanks to Pamela Kruger for her editorial contribution. Frank Comes, Joyce Barnathan, Christine Summerson, and Bob Dowling developed the series with our colleagues at our sister company, McGraw-Hill Professional—Philip Ruppel, Lisa Lewin, Mary Glenn, Herb Schaffner, and Ed Chupak. Very special thanks goes to Ruth Mannino for her excellent guidance on design and editorial production.

Stephen J. Adler
Editor-in-Chief
BusinessWeek

MARKETING
Power Plays

GEORGE BODENHEIMER: IN THE ESPN ZONE

© Courtesy of *BusinessWeek*.

POWER PLAYER

As rivals circle, ESPN boss George Bodenheimer is trying to push his world-beating brand even deeper into the lives of sports fans. He may not be a household name, but as president of ESPN Networks, he has quietly created one of the most powerful—and ubiquitous— media brands by moving aggressively into new markets.

This cover story from 2005 by Tom Lowry, with Mark Hyman, Ronald Grover, and Roger Crockett poses the question: Can Bodenheimer hold off his rivals?

Be willing to make big bets and push into new, unproven platforms before other competitors grab market share.

Know your brand. ESPN sees itself as the world's biggest sports fan and keeps its programming lively without taking itself too seriously.

Ensure that the brand maintains a clear, consistent message in all of its ventures.

Manage the organization as though it were a start-up, so that it remains agile and on the cutting edge.

Develop an inclusive culture. Your greatest talents may be working at the lowest levels, so make sure to give everyone a voice.

BEHIND THE SCENES POWERHOUSE

On September 19, 2005, millions of fans tuned in to a rare Monday night pro football doubleheader. Interlaced with plays were cutaways to a telethon to help victims of Hurricane Katrina. Viewers of ESPN and ABC saw some of the biggest legends in sports fielding calls from a studio in Manhattan's Times Square: Frank Gifford, Bart Starr, Gale Sayers, John Elway, Eric Dickerson, Donovan McNabb, George Bodenheimer . . . huh? George Boden-who?

What most folks who were watching didn't realize was that the stiff-looking guy with the phone in his ear is perhaps the single most influential person in all things sports. As president of the ESPN Networks and ABC Sports, George W. Bodenheimer runs one of the most successful and envied franchises in entertainment, the jewel of Walt Disney Company, and among the most powerful brands of the last quarter-century. While his round-the-clock networks are all about being brash and in-your-face, Bodenheimer is the rare media mogul who is adamant about staying behind the scenes. ESPN's top public relations executive had to practically drag Bodenheimer out of a production booth and push him in front of the cameras to make an appearance at the Katrina telethon, which he had helped to pull together with the National Football League in a matter of days. "It's just not about me," he could be heard mumbling as the PR chief made sure his tie was straight.

AGGRESSIVE PUSH INTO NEW MARKETS

That modesty has worked well for Bodenheimer, and ESPN has flourished during the seven years he has been at the helm. Sure, the ESPN he inherited had already extended itself from television to print, the Internet, and other platforms. And its smart-aleck, testosterone-laden culture was already a trademark. But Bodenheimer's vision of the company, where he started in the mailroom, is as a ubiquitous sports network—and more. To really understand ESPN, you need to see it as a cluster of feisty, creative enterprises under one killer brand. Its units, spread out mostly over offices in Connecticut, New York, and Los Angeles, act like start-ups, full of passionate staffers who are given the freedom to drive forward, but always with the mission of keeping the customers (rabid and tech-savvy fans like themselves) happy. Bodenheimer "realizes ESPN has to be fast-paced," says Simon

Williams, CEO of consultant Sterling Branding. "In his realm, if you stand still you're dead."

So, through 50 different businesses, Bodenheimer has pushed ESPN into broadband, on-demand video, wireless, high-definition, even books. His company has the X Games. It has burgers and fries at ESPN Zone restaurants. Video games are coming soon. All the while, the daily news and highlights show *SportsCenter* is as much must-see TV for millions of Americans as the nightly news shows were a generation ago. Put it all together, and Bodenheimer's competitors can't help but express awe. So ESPN has become a model for a wide range of companies, both inside and outside the media, that are struggling to make their brands work in new markets. "They have always had a halo to do things like a *SportsCenter* really well," says Jeff Price, chief marketing officer at *Sports Illustrated*. "Nobody has created those touchpoints with consumers like they have." Adds Adam Silver, the top TV executive at the National Basketball Association: "George lets others shine, but don't be fooled by the aw-shucks manner. He's an extremely effective manager who has put his company at the cutting edge of the digital revolution."

POWER MOVE

Many start-ups find that prosperity turns them into lumbering giants, always a step behind. With billions in revenues, and 50 different businesses, Bodenheimer has preserved its entrepreneurial energy by giving plenty of autonomy to managers so that they stay nimble.

AUTONOMY = AGILITY

Never one to gloat about his successes, the understated Bodenheimer confesses that the track he has been pounding is getting a whole lot steeper lately. At his back are a slew of rivals who are gaining momentum. First among them is Comcast, the number one U.S. cable operator. As well as looking to build a cable sports network to rival ESPN's, Comcast is also ESPN's biggest distributor, so its plans could aggravate what's already a delicate relationship. Bodenheimer has placed a hefty bet on an ESPN-branded cell phone and has said that making the new business a winner will be one of his biggest challenges. The cell phone is a move into an alluring market: delivering sports data and images to insatiable fans at all hours. But

POWER MOVE

ESPN has maintained its dominance by branching into a variety of platforms—before the competition takes hold. Equally key, audiences stay loyal because ESPN makes sure that all of the brand extensions keep its edgy, youthful voice and style.

the payoff is uncertain at best, and the venture could ultimately dent earnings and tarnish the brand. Launched in February 2005, it had signed up only about 10,000 customers as of May 2005. Bodenheimer's angst was turned up a notch or two higher when a key executive, Mark Shapiro, resigned in August 2005. As head of programming and production, Shapiro was seen as a driven ideas guy who kept new shows flowing and viewers tuning in. He was also an effective bad cop to Bodenheimer's good cop at the negotiating table.

Shapiro is often compared with Bodenheimer's high-energy predecessor, Steve Bornstein, ESPN's president during much of the 1990s. The 26-year-old network's initial blast of growth came under Bornstein, whose swagger infused the place with the cocky culture that is prevalent today. Bodenheimer's core strength, say longtime staffers, has been to preserve and encourage that vibe without making it all about George. His message to the staff is something like: ESPN isn't mine, it's yours, so run with it. And remember to have fun.

KNOW YOUR BRAND IDENTITY

Bodenheimer wears Brooks Brothers most days, but his operation is anything but buttoned-down. It's more about hoodies and DC skateboarding shoes, which is to say that it's all about being young. When *ESPN The Magazine* was launched in 1998, designer F. Darrin Perry gave its pages a bold look, with bright colors and unconventional type. That high-octane feel extends even to the magazine's offices in midtown Manhattan, which are designed to look like a gym, complete with an old school scoreboard. On any given day at the main ESPN campus in Bristol, Connecticut, now occupying 100 acres dotted with dozens of satellite dishes, you might find former All-Star second baseman and *Baseball Tonight* host Harold Reynolds waiting in line for brick-oven pizza in the fancy staff café, or *SportsCenter* anchor Stuart Scott looking for someone to spot him on the bench press in the state-of-the-art gym. A new $160 million digital center and studio, crammed full with robotic cameras and lighting rigs, is ringed with flat-screen TVs beaming sports in crisp hi-def. A central control room houses producers at computers editing a constant stream of digital-video game feeds.

The whole scene is NASA meets the bleacher creatures. "People have a passion for sports," says Rich Weinstein, the ESPN account director at ad agency Wieden+Kennedy, which has captured the spirit of ESPN through its award-winning spots for the network. "If your job is your passion, it brings a new perspective to the creative process. George was here when this was a start-up, and he has preserved that feeling." True to form, at a strategy session this summer for the new phone, the boss rolled up his sleeves, snapped open a Diet Coke, and burrowed down into every marketing idea the team pitched. Un-mogul-like, he never checked his BlackBerry or cut off discussion. Then he took the group out to a swanky trattoria.

A CULTURE OF INCLUSION

Bodenheimer, who squeezes in a golf game when he can, loves to break the ice by talking about—what else?—sports. He tries to stay engaged with workers across the company without micromanaging. "The great thing about George is that he can stand back and let his managers create," says Gary Hoenig, editor-in-chief of *ESPN The Magazine*. Going up against venerable *Sports Illustrated*, ESPN's seven-year-old biweekly has made great strides. Since 1999, circulation has grown by about 1 million, to 1.8 million, while *Sports Illustrated* has held steady at 3.3 million, according to the Audit Bureau of Circulations. Hoenig also credits Bodenheimer with giving him the freedom to develop lucrative specialty newsstand magazines, like one on fantasy football.

Tanya Van Court, whom Bodenheimer hired from Cablevision in April 2004 to oversee a revamping of broadband service, also insists that the boss never meddles. During the eight months that the new product ESPN360 was in development, "he would send hand-written notes with suggestions every week and a half or so," she

POWER MOVE

A key to long-term success is hiring employees who are committed to their work and to the corporate mission. To help attract and retain employees who share ESPN's passion for sports, the company has created office space that sports fans would love.

says. "He would offer up [notes like], 'make it the ultimate on-demand product for the sports fan and one that is as flexible as possible.'" When ESPN360 was launched in January 2005 with programming tailored for broadband—including short clips recapping Sunday games—it just may have hit on a new model. ESPN insiders liken it to cable TV in its infancy in the 1970s. So far, ESPN360 is available to nearly 5 million users through 14 different broadband providers.

TAPPING INNER STRENGTH

Can Bodenheimer the delegator and his decentralized, free-thinking culture keep up the winning streak? "The next two years will be a real big test for George," says Sean McManus, head of competing CBS Sports and a friend of Bodenheimer's. All around it, companies are imitating ESPN's cool and edgy packaging of sports. And if live sports is the last great mass market to lure advertisers, then how long can ESPN expect to dominate? Throw in a sports-crazed, often-elusive audience of young men bordering on the fanatic, and the economics are irresistible. That's why so many players are pushing into Bodenheimer's domain, from teams and leagues launching their own channels to cable and satellite operators creating new offerings. "ESPN listens to its audience very closely," says Sterling's Williams. "If it keeps doing that, [that] should be the glue that holds it together."

POWER MOVE

Replacing an accomplished CEO is never easy, and Bodenheimer's predecessor, Steve Bornstein, was a larger-than-life personality, credited with giving ESPN its DNA. Bodenheimer wisely managed, in his own low-key way, to tap the organization's inner strengths in order to build new successes.

Even so, the ESPN chief these days finds himself playing more defense than offense to keep games out of competitors' hands. One sign of the times: big hikes in the prices that ESPN is paying to lock up new pro football and Major League Baseball rights contracts. The $2.4 billion, eight-year MLB deal announced in September 2005 represents a 50 percent annual increase in fees. And in April 2005, ESPN ponied up $8.8 billion for a new eight-year *Monday Night Football* deal with the NFL for only one night of football. ABC will no longer broadcast games, including the lucrative Super Bowl; NBC grabbed ESPN's old Sunday night spot. The bottom line: ESPN will pay nearly twice as much a year than it did last time around, although other goodies were included, such as wireless rights that will allow ESPN to deliver Monday night highlights to cell phones for the first time. "You have to ask yourself how much growth will be left if they keep spending like this," says Richard Greenfield, an analyst at Fulcrum Global Partners LLC. Counters Bodenheimer: "Look, we are a sports-media company, and we program sports. It's like saying a seafood restaurant is being defensive when it reorders lobsters."

Bodenheimer, of course, lives in a world that's not totally of his own making. His ESPN is part of a tempest-rocked ship known as Disney. For years, ESPN has been able to do its own thing for one reason: it was the outfit that former CEO Michael D. Eisner could count on for the numbers. Now, with Eisner gone, Bodenheimer will be working closely with an old friend, new CEO Robert A. Iger, a one time exec at ABC Sports. The bond between Bodenheimer and Iger is strong, one pro league executive suggests, because they see themselves in each other—"two executives who have always been underestimated." Says Iger: "People sometimes mistake being polite for being easy. That's not the case with George. He's a man of great integrity, but he can be tough." Some speculate that Iger might eventually bring Bodenheimer to Burbank, but for now he needs his friend to stay put, keeping ESPN the financial bulwark it is to counterbalance the fickle businesses of theme parks and hit-driven TV and movies.

Indeed, ESPN revenues in 2005 were over $4 billion. The revenues—about 60 percent from distribution fees and 40 percent from advertising—represent about 15 percent of Disney's total. Analysts estimate that ESPN revenues could grow to nearly $6.8 billion in 2008. More important, ESPN is so central to cable menus that it gives Disney bargaining power with distributors to get them to pick up other Disney channels, be they SOAPnet or the ABC Family Channel. Emblematic of ESPN's clout, its longtime head of affiliate sales, Sean R. H. Bratches, was promoted in 2004 to oversee distribution for all of Disney's cable channels and broadband services. Using

POWER MOVE

Bodenheimer has made some big gambles that have yet to pay off. But in a fiercely competitive industry where companies are constantly trying to claim your turf, he understands that sometimes the biggest risk you can take is to not take a risk.

ESPN's leverage was a favorite tactic of Eisner's. So precious was ESPN to the Mouse House that the former CEO told investors several years ago: "We bought the ABC media network and ESPN for $19 billion in 1995. ESPN is worth substantially more than we paid for the entire acquisition."

NO RISK, NO REWARD

It's all the more remarkable, then, that ESPN was created with such modest intentions. It was founded in 1979 by former Hartford Whalers play-by-play man Bill Rasmussen on a patch of mud in the blue-collar central Connecticut town of Bristol by putting $9,000 on several credit cards. Rasmussen started the Entertainment and Sports Programming Network (ESPN) as a way to beam University of Connecticut Huskies games to a larger audience, using satellite dishes. But it soon became clear to Rasmussen and his son, Scott, that they were on to something with national potential. A year after Rasmussen put on the first shows, Getty Oil kicked in $100 million. Five years later, ABC bought out Getty's position (then owned by Texaco Inc.), and in 1988, Hearst Corp. bought a 20 percent position that was held at the time by RJR Nabisco. Hearst still has a 20 percent stake, but Disney is the active manager. "Nobody could have anticipated how much of a financial juggernaut ESPN would become," says Fulcrum analyst Greenfield.

Over the years, ESPN began to flex its muscles like the jocks it had helped turn into celebrities. It charged its cable and satellite distributors nearly twice as much for its service than any other channel fetched. (Today, ESPN gets an estimated $2.80 per subscriber per month, vs. about 40 cents for CNN, according to Morgan Stanley.) Double-digit hikes each year created a lot of ill will, culminating in a showdown two years ago that erupted in the halls of Congress. The battle pitted Bodenheimer against James O. Robbins, the outspoken CEO of cable operator Cox Communications Inc., who, acting on behalf of his industry, complained to lawmakers about the steep fees.

The brawl put Bodenheimer in an unwelcome spotlight, where he defended ESPN's pricing by blaming the high cost of rights deals with the leagues. Eventually Cox won lower annual fee increases, down from about 20 percent to about 7 percent. But ESPN claimed victory, too: New agreements included the operators' carriage of the latest ESPN channels, such as its Spanish-language outlet ESPN

Deportes. "We achieved everything we wanted in that negotiation," says Ed Durso, ESPN's top executive for government and public affairs. "George rose to the occasion."

PREPARE FOR BATTLE

Bodenheimer knows that the next battle will be the big one. News Corp. founder Rupert Murdoch, with 15 regional sports channels, is only making noises about a national sports channel. Comcast, however, is making plans. It has contacted ESPN executives about jumping ship, say sources close to both companies. Comcast already owns the Philadelphia 76ers, the Philadelphia Flyers, and a bunch of regional sports networks in cities from Philadelphia to Chicago to San Francisco. And it's no secret that Comcast CEO Brian L. Roberts and President Stephen B. Burke, a former Disney executive, want a piece of the ESPN business model. When the Philadelphia-based cable operator made its unsolicited $54 billion bid for Disney in February 2004, it was driven in part by a desire to capture ESPN.

Having its own hot sports channel would give Comcast ESPN-like leverage, amplifying its powerful 22 million subscriber base—even if its expertise is largely that of a distributor, not a programmer. For now, it's sticking to plans to convert its relatively unknown Outdoor Life Network, available in 64 million homes, into an ESPN for the new millennium. OLN got some buzz by airing Lance Armstrong's cycling feats in the Tour de France every summer. The rest of the channel's programming, from bull riding to fishing shows, has niche appeal at best.

But Comcast is moving fast. In the summer of 2005, it signed a $300 million, five-year deal to broadcast National Hockey League games on OLN starting that fall, with an option to bail out after two years. (ESPN ditched the sport after its contract expired in 2005 following the acrimonious lockout.) Now, Comcast needs to cinch some of the remaining 60 games available from MLB and win a package of Thursday and Saturday games from the NFL, which draws the largest TV audiences in sports. "Without the NFL, I don't see anybody being a threat to ESPN," says John Mansell, a senior analyst at Kagan Research LLC. Major League Baseball just awarded its remaining games to Fox and TBS. The NFL, in turn, awarded its remaining Thursday-Sunday game package essentially to itself for its cable outlet NFL Network.

TAKE THE PRODUCT TO YOUR CUSTOMER

Even as he fends off rivals, Bodenheimer is about to lead his troops into ESPN's trickiest brand extension so far. The idea is that ESPN could be missing the chance to stay in touch with fans who get up off the sofa or walk away from their computer screens. Says Bodenheimer: "We want fans to know you don't have to let the rest of your life get in the way of being a sports fan. You can take it with you." He met frequently with the Mobile ESPN development team to sign off on everything from the phone's black-and-red design on a Sanyo handset to the special displays constructed for big retailers. ESPN is leasing network time from Sprint Nextel Corp. and will outsource billing, messaging, and customer service (its price is yet to be announced). The opportunity to partner with ESPN was a no-brainer for Sprint Nextel CEO Gary Forsee. "As proud as we are of our brand, we'd be hard pressed to say Sprint can successfully go after the segments that ESPN [does]," he says. "But ESPN is the world leader, right?"

Still, the risk for ESPN is that if the phone bugs out, users won't be cursing some wireless outfit—they'll be blaming ESPN. "Content providers need to focus on what they do best," says one TV executive. "Hardware plays are fraught with problems." And the venture will require patience. "Sometimes it is up to two years with this kind of business before you reach enough scale with subscribers to be able to turn a profit," says Marina Amoroso, a wireless analyst with researcher Yankee Group. Bodenheimer says he's aware of the perils, "but it is a riskier move not to do this."

The last thing Bodenheimer needs now is to worry about top talent. Yet shortly before programming whiz Shapiro quit, chief marketing executive Lee Ann Daly resigned as well. Losing Shapiro, who quit in order to join Washington Redskins owner Dan Snyder in remaking Six Flags Inc., is the most problematic. Shapiro's handiwork is all over the network. ESPN Original Entertainment, the cable network's venture into movies, episodic dramas, and talk shows, was his creation. He gave juice to *Sports Century*, the Emmy Award–winning series of profiles of top athletes (and a horse, Secretariat).

In June 2005, Disney heaped new responsibility on Shapiro, promoting him to executive vice president, overseeing programming at both ESPN and ABC Sports. To all the world it looked as if his next step would be into headquarters. Then two months later, Shapiro met with Bodenheimer to tell him he was thinking about leaving. He'd had a feeler to head news operations at NBC. A few weeks later he accepted the offer from Snyder. "I knew at some point I was going to go entrepreneurial. It was just a question of when," says Shapiro.

Questions remain about why Bodenheimer and Iger waited so long to lock Shapiro into a new contract. But it is known that for some time, top executives at ESPN had been fielding complaints from the brass at pro sports leagues that they could no longer work with Shapiro. Several league officials said that they had never dealt with a negotiator who was so aggressive or so eager to pass himself off as the smartest guy at the table. "ESPN had just had tough relations with their customers, the cable guys," says one TV executive. "They could ill afford to have bad relations with their suppliers, too. They need the leagues." Shapiro shakes off such criticism. "Of course I'm going to be tough in negotiations. That's my job . . . not to say to [the leagues]: 'Here's a check, fill out how much you want.'" Still, by the end of Shapiro's tenure at ESPN, officials in at least two leagues refused to deal with him unless Bodenheimer was in on the talks.

DIRECT RELATIONSHIPS
Shapiro may have also ticked off Disney top brass in 2004 when he turned down an offer to become president of ABC Entertainment, the number two job under then-ABC executive Susan Lyne, who would have become chairperson, say sources within the company. The plan was to eventually move out Lyne and put Shapiro in charge, those sources say. Shapiro told Iger that he was excited about running prime time—but ultimately turned him down flat. Bodenheimer denies that there was any ill will toward Shapiro at Disney.

POWER MOVE

Staying in touch with what customers want can be a major challenge. Bodenheimer does his own informal market research, often leaving the luxury boxes at games to slip through the crowds and hear what sports fans are discussing.

Bodenheimer says he is confident that the culture he has fostered, one of tapping ESPN's inner strengths, will ultimately make Shapiro's departure less of a blow. "Mark was obviously a significant contributor," says Bodenheimer. "He's a great talent, but we have a tremendous reservoir of talent here." In fact, Bodenheimer used

Shapiro's departure to realign top management in early October into new segments: content, technology, sales and affiliates, and international. John Skipper, the much-admired senior executive who oversaw advertising and new media, now runs content, assuming much of Shapiro's programming mantle.

How Bodenheimer leads will go a long way in determining whether ESPN remains preeminent, especially as competitors zoom in on niches like volleyball, tennis, you name it. "ESPN will always be a general store of sports," says Brian Bedol, cofounder of college sports channel CSTV, "but it may have to learn to coexist with the leagues and new media companies [that] want to reach fans with very special interests. Technology today is allowing for a direct relationship with those fans."

Nobody wants to understand fans more than Bodenheimer, who often leaves the luxury boxes at games and walks through arenas studying the crowds—unrecognized, of course. "It's a minute-to-minute battle to retain viewers in today's media world," says Bodenheimer. "That's why I want to know what fans are saying—about sports, about ESPN." It's also why the most powerful man in sports needs to stay at the top of his game.

THE PROBLEM

Maintaining market leadership in a fast-changing industry that continually brings new, determined competitors

Finding a way to keep its hip and high-energy culture and brand identity as the company grows into a conglomerate

Following in the footsteps of a wildly successful leader who had a very different operating style

THE SOLUTION

Stay ahead of the pack by expanding and branching into new platforms.

Foster an entrepreneurial environment in which employees are given the latitude to think big and operate autonomously.

Make sure that the company stays on message in all of its products and enterprises.

Recognize the contributions that the departing executive made and build upon them, using your own management style.

SUSTAINING THE WIN

Embrace risk and move quickly to implement new ideas that can help the company broaden its reach and attract more consumers in different markets.

JAMES OWENS: CATERPILLAR SINKS ITS CLAWS INTO SERVICES

© Courtesy of BusinessWeek.

POWER PLAYER

Caterpillar is achieving record profits, so why is CEO James W. Owens so intent on expanding into new markets? Because expansion is the only way to continue to thrive in a cyclical industry. Cat's ambitious growth target is $50 billion in revenue by 2010. It plans to hit that mark with the help of its services divisions.

In this December 2005 story, Michael Arndt looks at Caterpillar's growth during a possible downturn.

Anticipate and plan for slowdowns, even when a company is thriving.

Identify and expand into hidden opportunities for growth, untapped markets that could provide long-term profits.

Bolster even the strongest divisions so that they can withstand the market challenges that will be coming in the future.

Focus on new opportunities for growth in areas of brand expertise.

REFILL YOUR BUCKET BEFORE IT'S EMPTY

Jennifer South aims her needle gun at a broken-down engine and blasts away. The giant 12-cylinder motor had powered a mining truck until a few weeks earlier, when it was carted off to Caterpillar Inc.'s remanufacturing plant in Corinth, Mississippi, to be salvaged. Over its brutal life, the engine had become caked with dust that had hardened like concrete. Now, wearing safety glasses, earplugs, gloves, and a protective apron, South must chisel away the years of buildup to unearth a bolt so that she can further dismantle the 17,800-pound carcass of iron and steel. The air-driven gun pecks at the encrusted engine, with rods that look like knitting needles, until the calcification is gone.

"It's oily, greasy, heavy work," says South, who joined the company nine years ago as a 19-year-old college student. And progress is slow. The plant's 600 employees disassemble and rebuild an average of just two diesel engines per eight-hour shift, cleaning, inspecting, and repairing 20,000 parts along the way. But multiply that output by Caterpillar's other remanufacturing plants—the company will start up its fourteenth, in Shanghai, in early 2006—and then multiply that by the five-figure price of these reclaimed products, and it gets easier to see why the division has become Caterpillar's fastest-growing unit this decade. Annual revenue tops $1 billion and is estimated to grow 20 percent a year.

This type of unglamorous, quintessentially old-economy dirty work is how CEO James W. Owens is planning to make Caterpillar a $50 billion company. His strategy: have service businesses refill the bucket when the current manufacturing gusher inevitably begins to slow.

A 33-year Caterpillar veteran, Owens, 59, ascended to the top job in early 2004. Since then, his biggest problem has been simply keeping pace with the upsurge in demand for earthmoving equipment and heavy-duty engines. That "yellow iron," as

POWER MOVE

When a company is on top, it is tempting to just maintain the status quo. But Owens is planning ahead for the inevitable slump, convincing dealers to order less and diminish their inventories. While this will lower current sales it will increase them later when demand for Cat's products ebbs.

Owens calls it, helped Cat reach No. 23 on the *BusinessWeek* 50 tally of 2004's best corporate performers.

TAPPING NEW MARKETS

But Caterpillar's basic business is extraordinarily cyclical, as Owens, a Ph.D. economist, knows all too well. Behind today's turbocharged results, another industrial bust may already be in the offing. In fact, Owens believes that the domestic market for big-rig truck engines is at its peak now. The mining sector will top out in 2009 if not sooner, he adds, with an outright recession possible as soon as 2011.

To offset the slowdown, Owens wants to make more acquisitions, particularly in fast-growing markets such as China, and to double the pace of new rollouts to grab market share. He's also pushing dealers to cut inventories. That will reduce orders now, but it should keep factories busier when retail sales slacken. And for as long as demand holds up, he's hiking prices.

Services, however, are the key to Cat's strategic shift. The Peoria (Illinois) company has three service divisions today—Financial Services, Logistics, and Remanufacturing—which account for 15 percent of its revenues and perhaps 20 percent of its net income. Because of their fast growth, Owens says, these divisions should generate 20 percent of sales by 2010, which would put the troika's combined revenues at $10 billion. Since these also are higher-margin businesses, their bottom-line contribution should increase even more, to as much as 30 percent by the end of the decade, calculates Ann Duignan, an analyst with Bear, Stearns & Co. Inc.

Cat Financial extends credit for three-quarters of all Caterpillar sales, so it has soared right along with the equipment business. The division, which averages 95,000 customers a year, opened its first office in China in 2005. It's no surprise, then, that it's having a record year, with expected revenues of $2.3 billion and a $350 million profit. Cat Logistics, meanwhile, is prized for its steady income stream. The unit warehouses and delivers

POWER MOVE

Many firms have tried to make a splash by chasing after what's "hot," losing countless millions in the process. Cat, however, has been proudly boosting its bottom line by expanding into a distinctly unexciting, but highly lucrative industry: remanufacturing engine parts.

replacement parts for 60 industrial customers, including Bombardier Inc. and Harley-Davidson, Inc. In October it signed a contract with General Motors Europe that will pay out nearly $100 million a year over 10 years.

The remanufacturing division is the newest of the service units. Caterpillar got into the business almost by accident: it dates back to a favor that Cat reluctantly did for Ford Motor Company in 1973. To lower its own costs, Ford's truckmaking subsidiary wanted a source of rebuilt engines, which generally sell for half the price of new ones.

POWER MOVE

Frequently, companies are faced with a client that demands a service that could be seen as just unpleasant drudgery. When Ford Motor Company insisted that Cat begin making rebuilt engines for Ford's trucks, it did the job and had the vision to see—and seize—the market opportunity in the dreaded task.

As Caterpillar executives tell it, management saw Ford's demand as a chore. But because supplying Ford with new engines would be such a moneymaker, the company consented and opened a repair shop in Bettendorf, Iowa. By 1982 the business had grown enough that Caterpillar bought a vacant factory in Corinth, Mississippi, to reclaim used crankshafts. Still, even into the late 1990s, after Caterpillar built a second plant in Nuevo Laredo, Mexico, and a third in Prentiss, Mississippi, remanufacturing was considered a sideline. "It was something we had to do," recalls Steven L. Fisher, president of the division.

STAY ALERT FOR HIDDEN OPPORTUNITIES

In 2000, management realized that this handful of ancillary factories represented a hidden opportunity. The business had become reliably profitable, and the marketplace was full of mom-and-pop outfits, making it easy for the company to pick up business through acquisitions. Caterpillar's own numbers argued for expansion, too. As orders for new equipment were falling amid a plunge in the industrial economy, revenues and profits from Caterpillar services continued to climb. Since then, as the company has built and acquired more facilities, Cat Remanufacturing's results have doubled.

The division's flagship plant in Corinth, about 100 miles east of Memphis, extracts every last bit of value from used parts. The facility, which is the size of six football fields, is a cacophony of industrial clangs and whirs as workers strip old engines down to their individual components and then, after salvaging whatever they can, put them all back together. No piece is too inconsequential for recycling. In the area where Jennifer South works, employees fill wire bins with bolts, nuts, and washers sorted by stock-keeping unit number. The parts are then cleansed in a bath of molten salt to come out looking like new.

Nor are damaged goods automatically tossed aside as scrap. Down the line, a computerized machine builds up a worn-down engine block by spraying it with a fine mist of liquefied metal. When it's done, the surface has been raised by the width of a dime. Other workers dust engine blocks, crankshafts, and other major components with a metal powder that, when magnetized and viewed under ultraviolet light, can expose otherwise invisible cracks. Like dentistry on a large scale, these cracks then are dug out, and the cavities are filled by hand with iron and machine-polished to original product specifications.

FOCUS ON GROWTH

Analysts praise the unit because it allows Caterpillar to profit again and again from the same goods. By selling rebuilt products at discount prices, it keeps makers of knockoff parts out of the lucrative aftermarket. And the business seems to have room to grow: Caterpillar's Shanghai plant will let it offer rebuilt parts in China, a market that could be big, since few customers there can afford new equipment. Remanufacturing, says Owens, "has the highest growth and earnings potential of any of our businesses in the next five years."

> POWER MOVE
>
> Diversifying can buffer a company during downturns, and Owens has been astute in focusing on expanding Cat's services division, which has the most potential for growth, and moving fast into China, a huge, untapped market for remanufactured parts.

Owens is confident of maximizing that potential. During the next contraction, he's promising that earnings won't drop below $2.50 a share, as they did in 2001 and 2002. The only way he can meet that commitment, says Bear Stearns' Duignan, is if his services strategy pans out as planned.

MONDAY MORNING...

THE PROBLEM
Maintaining steady success in an intensely cyclical industry

Finding and developing new markets that will complement existing businesses and ensure that the firm continues to grow

THE SOLUTION
Expand the ancillary, even minor services popular with customers that the company already offers.

Take actions that may reduce sales in the short term if this will protect the company during recessions.

Corner the market on products that are reliably profitable, even if they are "boring" and unglamorous.

SUSTAINING THE WIN
Keep a laser focus on not only what the business needs to be successful today, but also what it will need to withstand the market challenges of tomorrow.

STEVEN FREIBERG:
THINKING LOCALLY AT CITIGROUP

©Todd France

Move quickly to
expand the
company's reach by
building new offices
and making
acquisitions.

Find creative ways to
fully mine the
spending power of
the organization's
regular customers.

Focus on improving
customer service—
and promoting
improved service—
to entice current
customers to buy
more products and
services.

POWER PLAYER

Citibank may be the second
largest bank in the world, but the
global giant is in trouble at home,
rapidly losing market share to U.S.
rivals. Steve Freiberg, co-head of
Citi's Global Consumer Group,
North America, plans to turn
the company around with a
deceptively simple strategy:
focusing on the consumer.

Mara Der Hovanesian's 2005 profile of Steve
Freiberg looks at the strategy behind improving
domestic growth.

NEW FOCUS ON ORGANIC GROWTH

Like politics, all banking is local—even for mighty Citigroup. While Citi's $1.5 trillion in assets make it the world's second biggest bank, U.S. retail operations are hurting. Basically, Citi is being left in the dust by aggressive and expansion-minded rivals. Its 3.4 percent share of nationwide deposits is just over one-third of the acquisitive Bank of America Corp.'s 9.8 percent share, for example. Last year, that widening gap pushed Citi out of the catbird seat it has occupied for years as the world's largest bank as measured by deposits. And its revenues of about $15 billion from U.S. retail banking were flat in the first half, while BofA raked in a record $14 billion, up 23 percent.

Citi's domestic problems run deep. Most of its 34 million customers buy fewer products or services, such as credit cards, mortgages, or checking accounts, than clients at rivals like BofA or Wells Fargo & Company, which makes Citi less profitable. It's a lowly seventh in the giant mortgage and home-equity business, about one-third the size of market leader Washington Mutual, Inc. Citi's retail bank is limited in its geographic reach, and U.S. credit card account growth has stagnated. The result: a global institution that is essentially a New York bank at home, with 60 percent of its deposits coming from the region—and one with a reputation for "below average" customer service, according to financial consultants A. T. Kearney. Says Merrill Lynch & Co., Inc. bank analyst Guy Moszkowski: "They are very clearly getting upstaged in the United States. If they don't find a way to grow faster, or if the business shrinks because of competition, that's a big problem."

> **POWER MOVE**
>
> Even large organizations can become provincial and find themselves limited geographically. Steve Freiberg understands the danger and is undertaking an aggressive expansion effort. Not only has the bank constructed new domestic branches—23 in one year, vs. just 22 in the prior seven years—but it also is acquiring small banks in fast-growing areas, such as Texas and California.

The task of kicking up growth falls to Steven J. Freiberg. In August 2005, Chief Executive Charles O. Prince picked him to head Citi's retail banking operations in the United States and Canada, newly carved out from the global bank. In the old days, Citi would have bought growth with a few big deals. But Freiberg doesn't have that option. The Federal Reserve, leery of Citi's series of worldwide regulatory run-ins since 2002, has banned the bank from making major acquisitions for now. "If we're going to grow, we can't rely mainly on the old acquisition model anymore. We are taking a much more focused view of organic growth," says Freiberg.

GETTING MORE FROM YOUR BASE

As he sees it, Citi has plenty of customers. He mainly needs them to buy more stuff. So Freiberg's first big push is to mine the bank's 120 million credit card customers—along with 18 million new ones annually—for more business. If he can sell at least one bank product to 1 in 20 of them, he says he can double the retail bank's profits. Also, Freiberg wants to step up marketing to professionals such as doctors and lawyers, as well as to small-business owners and CitiGold bank customers. These so-called mass affluent clients with at least $100,000 in assets are a potential gold mine. He figures that every new product they buy, say an auto loan or a mortgage, yields 12 times the profits of the first sale simply because the cost of recruiting new customers is so high.

Slow growth in deposits may crimp Freiberg's ambitions. Citi ranks seventh, behind BofA, Wachovia Corporation, JPMorgan Chase & Co., and Washington Mutual, in retail deposit growth for the last 12 months, according to SNL Financial in Charlottesville, Virginia.

This matters because deposits are the launchpad for more lucrative customer relationships. At BofA, which has the largest market share, more than half of its customers buy more than one product. Only one in five do so at Citi, according to Prudential Financial, Inc., bank analyst Michael Mayo. Because the bank has underinvested in recruiting and training, customer service—and thus deposit growth—has suffered. "Retail banking economics are overwhelmingly dominated

Citibank already has lots of customers— some 34 million of them. The problem is that their customers haven't been buying enough bank products. So Freiberg is targeting the bank's big spenders— professionals with $100,000 or more in assets—using new technology to track them and offering discounts and other incentives to spend more.

by deposits," says James M. McCormick, president of First Manhattan Consulting Group in New York.

ORGANIZE SALES AROUND CUSTOMERS NOT PRODUCTS

Freiberg has been in tight spots before. When he joined Citi's credit card group in 1997, most Americans were charging up a storm on bank cards, but Citi's business had plunged 25 percent in a year. A 25-year Citi vet who often lands turnaround assignments, Freiberg slashed costs and built new models to manage credit risk. He kicked sales into gear with direct mail, preapproved credit cards—a marketing tactic pioneered by his group that now is standard industry practice. He also built the largest U.S. private-label card business by acquiring the portfolios of Federated Department Stores, Inc., Sears, Roebuck and Co., and Home Depot, Inc. In 2005, cards earned $4 billion, nearly a quarter of Citi's total profits and 10 times more than when Freiberg arrived.

Just six weeks into his new job, Freiberg made some big changes. He restructured the group and created three positions to run distribution, technology, and franchise management. Ray Quinlan, a former executive vice president at Citigroup Mergers & Acquisitions, now heads retail distribution. His mission: to weld Citi's 130,000 Primerica brokers, 2,200 consumer finance offices, and 884 retail bank branches into a cohesive sales operation. One of Citi's big problems has been that sales and support staff have been organized around products rather than customers. "It's pretty clear that Citi's various consumer businesses in the United States have not been integrated in a management or information sense," says Bear Stearns & Co. Inc. bank analyst David Hilder.

> Believing that Citi's mistake was that it focused too much on product lines and not enough on North American customers, Freiberg immediately created three new positions to run distribution, technology, and franchise management. Equally important, he is pushing to unite the company's brokers, retail bank branches, and consumer finance offices so that they function as a cohesive sales operation.

THANKS TO THE CUSTOMER

In the future, high-end customers will be more cosseted. The effort will be based on an existing rewards program, the ThankYou Network, that lets card and bank customers accumulate points to redeem for purchases at merchants such as Home Depot or Bed Bath & Beyond Inc. Freiberg plans to use technology to track these loyal customers and ply them with discounts and other incentives to buy extra Citi products and services. He's also introducing new cards. On October 17, Citi planned to launch the annual- and late-fee-free Simplicity Card.

For Citi, known for its "below average" customer service, improvement is a necessity. The key: investment in training of the rank and file. Wells Fargo has done this and found that some 40 percent of its retail sales come through its bank tellers.

Freiberg's effort to attract and retain customers will extend to Citi's retail and consumer finance branches as well. Citi built 23 new branches in 2005, vs. just 22 in the prior seven years. Still, Freiberg must quicken his pace. Chase, for one, will have built 150 new branches nationwide by year-end. Citi will also have to train branch staff to develop stronger ties to customers. At Wells Fargo, which has done this for years, some 40 percent of all retail sales come through one of its 25,000 tellers. Wells says that this source of sales helps it sell an industry-leading average of four products to each customer. Says SNL financial analyst Eric Reinford: "Citi is still playing catch-up to the retail boom of the 2000s that everyone else has been cashing in on."

The timing of Freiberg's push is tricky. Citi may be investing big in retail just as U.S. consumers' spending habits shift. The mortgage business is cooling, and many are burdened by credit card debt. In any case, what's happening is a radical change for Citi. By creating Freiberg's position and splitting off domestic banking, Prince broke with Sanford I. Weill's centralized strategy of treating Citi's consumer operations as a global enterprise. While the consumer business overseas is growing at a fast clip, Prince saw that North American retail banking was a separate challenge. As he handed over Citi's lackluster domestic retail operations to Freiberg, Prince tried to brace him for the worst, warning: "Yours is the harder job."

MONDAY MORNING...

THE PROBLEM

Recapturing a market that is being taken over by aggressive competitors

Ensuring your most profitable customers continue to buy the right products and services

THE SOLUTION

Define your top priorities and be willing to restructure to achieve new goals.

Identify the most profitable customers and offer them inducements to buy more products and services.

Boost the company's presence by acquiring small companies in high-growth areas.

SUSTAINING THE WIN

Maintain a vigorous search for untapped opportunities to increase sales.

Maintain vigorous emphasis on customer service.

PAUL OTELLINI:
INSIDE INTEL

©Kim Kulish / Corbis

POWER PLAYER

When CEO Paul Otellini unveiled his plan to reinvent Intel, the company was raking in big profits. But Otellini saw that the market was changing and for the chipmaker to continue to grow, it had better change too. Otellini took measures to revitalize the company.

In this early 2006 profile by Cliff Edwards, we learn CEO Paul Otellini's bold plan is to blow up the brand and reshape the company.

Be ready to challenge and change a "successful culture." What was innovative in the past does not reflect new market wants and needs.

Reevaluate and be ready to overhaul virtually every aspect of the business in order to transform the company.

Update the company's image—including its logo, tag line, and ad campaign—so that the public receives a clear, positive message about the brand.

Seek out partners that can advance the organization's strategy and help it reach its goals.

Keep in mind that the best marketed technology can beat the best technology.

THE COURAGE TO BLOW UP THE BRAND

Even the gentle clinking of silverware stopped dead. Andrew S. Grove, the revered former Intel Corp. chief executive and now a senior adviser to the company, had stepped up to the microphone in a hotel ballroom down the street from Intel's Santa Clara, California, headquarters, preparing to respond to a startling presentation by new Chief Marketing Officer Eric B. Kim. All too familiar with Grove's legendary wrath, many of the 300 top managers at the 2005 gathering tensed in their seats as they waited for a tongue-lashing of epic proportions. "No one knew what to think," recalls one attendee.

> Otellini didn't wait until Intel was in crisis to reshape the company's mission. He saw that demand for its microprocessors—its main product—was slowing down and would probably continue to do so, as the public's use of technology was changing.

The reason? Kim's plan, cooked up with the new CEO, Paul S. Otellini, was a sharp departure from the company that Grove had built. Essentially, Kim and Otellini were proposing to blow up Intel's brand, the fifth-best-known in the world. As Otellini looked on from a front table, Kim declared that Intel must "clear out the cobwebs" and kill off many Grove-era creations. Intel Inside? Dump it, he said. The Pentium brand? Stale. The widely recognized dropped "e" in Intel's corporate logo? A relic.

Grove's deep baritone, sharpened by the accent of his native Hungary, pierced the expectant silence. But instead of smiting the Philistines, Intel's patriarch sprinkled holy water on Otellini's plan. He understood that it was not a repudiation of him, but rather a recognition that times had changed—and that Intel needed to change with them. "I want to say," he boomed, "that this program strikes me as one of the best manifestations incorporating Intel values of risk taking, discipline, and results orientation I have ever seen here. I, for one, fully support it."

As the executives rose to greet him with relieved applause, the moment signaled a historic shift for one of the world's most powerful technology companies. Intel would leave the Grove era behind and head into uncharted territory. Otellini unveiled the new strategy and new products in January 2006, at the Consumer Electronics

Show in Las Vegas. Central to the effort is the first new corporate logo in more than three decades and a $2.5 billion advertising and marketing blitz.

NEW MARKETS, NEW MODELS

The changes go far deeper than the company's brand. Under Grove and his successor, Craig R. Barrett, Intel thrived by concentrating on the microprocessors that power personal computers. By narrowing the company's focus, the duo buried the competition. They invested billions in hyperproductive plants that could crank out more processors in a day than some rivals did in a year. Meanwhile, they helped give life to the Information Age with ever-faster, more powerful chips.

Otellini is tossing out the old model. Instead of remaining focused on PCs, he's pushing Intel to play a key technological role in a half-dozen fields, including consumer electronics, wireless communications, and health care. And rather than just focusing on microprocessors, he wants Intel to create all kinds of chips and software as well, and then meld them together into what he calls "platforms." The idea is to power innovation from the living room to the emergency room. "This is the right thing for our company, and to some extent the industry," he says. "All of us want [technology] to be more powerful and to be simpler, to do stuff for us without us having to think about it."

Why the shift? Stark necessity. PC growth is slowing, and cell phones and handheld devices are competing for the *numero uno* spot in people's lives. Otellini must either reinvent Intel or face a future of creaky maturity. Revenue growth has averaged 13 percent for the past three years, but analysts believe that Intel will see only 7 percent growth in 2006, to $42.2 billion. Meantime, profits, which have surged an average 40 percent annually over the past three years, are expected to rise a measly 5 percent, to $9.5 billion. "It's a race

In an era in which consumers are inundated with media messages, brands must have a clear, distinct identity if they are to stand out. As a result, Otellini revamped the company logo for the first time in more than 30 years, added a new tag line, and staged a splashy event at the Consumer Electronics Show to kick off the advertising and marketing blitz.

for Intel and other companies to figure out how fast its revenue is going to come from emerging areas before PC margins begin to come down sharply," says Ragu Gurumurthy, head of technology practice for Boston tech consultancy, Adventis Corp.

BLOW UP THE CULTURE

Intel has tried entering new markets in the past, particularly under Barrett. Yet it always treated them as tangential and never let them detract from the core processor effort. Not anymore. Otellini, who took over as CEO in May 2005, has reorganized the company from top to bottom, putting most of its 98,000 employees into new jobs. He created business units for each product area, including mobility and digital health, and scattered the processor experts among them. He has also added 20,000 people in the past year. The result? Intel is poised to launch more new products in 2006 than at any time in its history.

Intel's culture is changing, too. Under the charismatic Grove, who was CEO from 1987 to 1998 and then chairman until 2005, the company was a rough-and-tumble place. Grove's motto was "Only the paranoid survive," and managers frequently engaged in "constructive confrontation," which any outsider would call shouting. Engineers ruled the roost. Grove and Barrett also instituted the practice of doling out cash to PC makers for joint advertising, which Intel's rivals have alleged blocks them from some markets.

Otellini is more diplomatic, partly by nature and partly by necessity. An intensely private man in his mid-50s, he rarely reveals irritation—and when he does, it's with a slight frown. His management mantra: "Praise in public, criticize in private."

He is also the first nonengineer to run the company. Otellini studied economics in college at the University of San Francisco and joined Intel in 1974, straight out of business school at the University of California at Berkeley. Many of the new employees he's bringing on board also aren't typical Intel hires. They include

POWER MOVE

Like so many successful companies, Intel developed a proud corporate culture, with an ingrained way of thinking and doing business. To challenge that, Otellini hired executives from outside the company and placed them in key positions, knowing that they would bring a fresh perspective and be willing to question the status quo.

software developers, sociologists, ethnographers, and even doctors to help develop products. He lays particular emphasis on marketing expertise because he thinks that the only way Intel can succeed in new markets is by communicating more clearly what the technology can do for customers. "To sell technology now, you have to do it in a way where it's much more simple," says Otellini. "You can't talk about the bits and the bytes."

NO GLITZ, NO GLORY

The changes have created some angst among employees. In particular, many high-level engineers working on PC products feel that they've been stripped of their star status. "The desktop group used to rule the company, and we liked it that way," says one former chip designer, adding that some engineers now feel "directionless." Other employees are simply uncomfortable with the new emphasis on marketing. "There definitely are people who are highly skeptical, who think this is all fluff, all just gloss—that if you make good technology, you don't need the glitz," says Genevieve Bell, an in-house ethnographer who researches how people in emerging markets like China and India use technology.

Widespread change can't be simply dictated from above; management needs to get "buy-in" from employees. Intel's management has repeatedly spelled out the new vision, and Otellini has made an effort to show that he cares, touring offices and talking to workers when their managers weren't around.

Yet Intel and Otellini aren't shying away from glitz these days. For its bash at the Consumer Electronics Show in 2005, the company booked the hip-hop band Black Eyed Peas, with its hit *Let's Get It Started*. Beforehand, Otellini unveiled the new Intel during his keynote speech. It started with a whole new look for the 37-year-old company. The Intel Inside logo disappeared, replaced by an updated Intel logo with a swirl around it to signify movement. For the first time since the early 1990s, the company added a tag line: "Leap ahead."

Meanwhile, the famous Pentium brand will be slowly phased out. In its place will be a troika of brands, two of them freshly minted. Viiv (rhymes with "alive") is the name of a new chip for home PCs, designed to replace your TiVo, your stereo, and, potentially, your cable or satellite set-top box. It will be able to download first-run movies, music, and games and shift them around the home. Intel also will launch a set of notebook PC chips under the three-year-old Centrino brand, as well as so-called dual-core chips, which will put two processor cores on one sliver of silicon. The new brand "Core" will be put on products that don't meet the specifications of the Viiv or Centrino platforms. The effort is winning high-profile support. In January, Apple Computer Inc., which had never before used Intel's chips, became one of the first companies to offer products with the dual-core chips.

POWER MOVE

Intel's culture had been so dominated by engineers (and so hostile to marketers) that Otellini didn't just move most employees into new jobs to learn new ways of working. He also mandated that employees work in teams, forcing staffers to work with people from a variety of backgrounds, from medicine to marketing.

SHAKE IT UP BEFORE THE CRISIS HITS

One of Otellini's key steps in all this was hiring Kim away from Samsung Group a year ago. Kim had led Samsung's marketing since 1999 and helped build the Korean maker of consumer electronics, cell phones, and computer chips into a hot global brand. But Otellini didn't just swipe a major talent from the company that's increasingly seen as Intel's prime competitor. By hiring an outsider who reports directly to the CEO for the first time in Intel's history, Otellini also got someone who could play bad cop and push through unpopular changes when necessary. Rank-and-file employees grumble about Kim and what they consider his autocratic style, but he makes no apologies. "I tell people they're not just about making silicon. They're helping people's lives improve, and we need to let the world know that," says Kim.

Yet such a transformation is a daunting task, especially for a company that has never had much success outside the computer industry. Companies that have been good at transforming themselves, from Nissan and Apple to Texas Instruments, typically need a crisis to precipitate change, says management expert Jay R. Galbraith of Galbraith Associates. And although Intel is facing a possible slowdown, it's still pulling in nearly $1 billion a month in profits. "Change is really hard when you're solidly on top," says Galbraith. "He'll have to bring in new people who have new skill sets."

MARKET-FOCUSED PRODUCT DEVELOPMENT

Competitors keep nipping at Intel's heels. In 2003, long-time rival Advanced Micro Devices Inc. launched its Opteron and Athlon 64 chips, outgunning Intel in both raw power and lower power consumption. AMD's market share rose to 17.8 percent last quarter, up from 16.6 percent in early 2003, and some analysts predict that it will continue gaining share until Intel fields competitive chips in late 2007. AMD CEO Hector J. de Ruiz equates Intel's position with that of American automakers, scrambling to find innovation even as consumers flock to Japanese rivals. "People are smart enough to pick quality when given a choice, and calling something a platform doesn't guarantee quality," Ruiz says.

If a leader wants to alter the DNA of an organization—not just some of its business practices—then there can be no sacred cows. So Intel is reevaluating even its legendary tight alliance with Microsoft, questioning whether it will continue to use Microsoft's Windows operating system on its Viiv machines.

In the cell phone market, Texas Instruments and Qualcomm Inc. have held fast against Intel's incursions. Intel Executive Vice President Sean M. Maloney once wore snowshoes to a company sales conference to illustrate the deep slog. In 2006, AMD and TI plan to field their own chip platforms aimed at capturing some real estate in the digital home.

So Otellini is shaking things up throughout the company. In addition to the reorganization, he's making big changes in the way products are developed. While in the past engineers worked on ever-faster chips and then let marketers try to sell them, there are now teams of people with a cross section of skills. Chip engineers, software developers, marketers, and market specialists all work together to come up with compelling products.

One example of the new approach is Bern Shen. A doctor who practiced internal medicine for 15 years, he joined Intel three months ago to help develop technologies for digital health. He works with Intel's ethnographers to figure out which technologies might help in monitoring the vital signs of the elderly or tracking the diets of people with Alzheimer's. "The fact that they hired me is an indication of the new Intel," he says.

Otellini is convinced that such collaboration will lead to breakthrough innovations. He imagines a day when people will use Centrino laptops to watch live TV on the subway and kids will be able to download *Spider-Man 3* to their home theater on the same day it's released worldwide. Shen's work could lead to Intel technology that allows the elderly to keep living at home, even as data on their vital signs are zapped to doctors several times a day. "This is the right model," Otellini says. "Now it's just a matter of playing it out."

> Creating innovative products requires a willingness to use unorthodox tactics to track evolving consumer tastes. For instance, for the first time in its history, Intel is hiring ethnographers to study how people use its—and its rivals'—products.

THE VISION TO PUSH INNOVATIVE APPROACHES

If the world buys Otellini's ideas, industries from Hollywood to health care could be turned upside down. The media and entertainment industries may be forced to rethink their business models. The health-care industry could be transformed, with doctors diagnosing or even treating patients remotely. "The most important thing about Intel is that they've got the vision," says Russ Bodoff, executive director of the Center for Aging Services Technologies, a coalition of 400 companies, universities, and hospitals. "They are pushing some very innovative approaches in areas that relate to dementia, Alzheimer's care, and Parkinson's disease."

The ultimate goal: to provide the manufacturers of everything from laptops and entertainment PCs to cell phones and hospital gear with complete packages of chips and software. The template is Centrino. When Otellini was leading product planning in the core PC business from 1998 to 2002, he decided that rather than just roll out another fast processor, he would bundle it with a relatively new wireless Internet technology called Wi-Fi. The combo made it a breeze for people to connect to the Net from airport lounges and coffee shops. Backed with an initial $300 million marketing campaign, Centrino notebooks became an instant hit, revitalizing the PC market and persuading consumers to snap up the higher-margin products.

CHANGE THE ENGINE MIDFLIGHT

Still, Intel's first big success in diversification was only a half-step away from the core PC market. Will it be able to do as well in other areas? Consider Viiv. In the consumer electronics market, where Viiv devices will be positioned as an all-in-one DVD player, game console, TiVo, and music jukebox, it faces plenty of big-name competitors. Meanwhile, brand-new challengers are appearing on the horizon. Sony Corp., with its PlayStation, aims to offer games, movies, and music on the device, which uses chips from IBM. Cable and satellite providers such as Comcast Corp. and DirecTV Group Inc. are adding more features and services to their set-top boxes, such as on-demand television shows and XM satellite radio.

> To succeed in a competitive economy, even corporate giants must be prepared to become humble collaborators. Intel is partnering with major Hollywood players and music services, as well as with Apple, a company that Intel once dismissed.

The need to cut through the clutter of competitive activity is why Otellini and Kim have lifted branding to new heights at Intel. But for a huge company like Intel, it will be especially tough. "In many ways, it's like trying to change the engines on an airplane when you're flying it," says Russ Meyer, chief strategy officer for branding consultancy, Landor Associates. Companies must try not only to differentiate themselves from competitors but also to align internally to make sure the same message is clear to employees. For an "ingredient" brand like Intel with no products that a consumer actually can pick up from the local Best Buy or Wal-Mart , the trick also is to convince new customers of the value of using its products.

With that in mind, Otellini's Digital Home team has struck some of the biggest content deals to date with major Hollywood players and music services to entice both customers and consumers to the Viiv platform. The hundreds of millions it will dole out for marketing Viiv have partners like Sony and Philips Electronics salivating. They also seem to be genuinely impressed with the new attitude at Otellini's Intel. "I have seen more flexibility, more of an open mindset than in years past," says Sony Vice President Mike Abary, who heads the company's Vaio PC business. "They realize that times have changed, that they don't have all the answers. So it has been much more collaborative working with them."

THINK OUT OF THE BOX

Otellini also has gone to great lengths to win over marketing maestro Steve Jobs. It's quite a reversal. For years, Grove and Barrett pooh-poohed Apple as a niche company whose products had sleek form, but nowhere near the function of computers with Intel's chips. Yet Otellini set about wooing Jobs almost from the start. In June 2005, a month after Otellini took over, the two companies announced that Apple would begin shipping Macs and other products with Intel chips inside in 2006. Otellini aims to use the Apple relationship to force PC makers to step up their innovation. "They've always been a front-runner in design," he says. "As they start taking advantage of some of our lower-power products, that form factor will improve significantly. I think it will help drive a trend toward smaller, cheaper, cooler."

Jobs's influence extends beyond design. At Otellini's urging, Apple's "Think Different" vernacular is beginning to take root inside Intel. The two chief executives also appear to be developing a real friendship. Intel insiders say they talk regularly. And when Prince Charles and his wife, Camilla, visited Silicon Valley in late November 2005, Jobs and Otellini were side by side, hobnobbing with the royals.

The Apple relationship could create some strain with Intel's two old *compadres* in the PC business, Dell and Microsoft. Dell has been one of Intel's most loyal customers; it's the only major U.S. maker of PCs that hasn't come out with boxes powered by AMD chips. So if Intel provides strong support for Apple in the PC business, it could prompt Dell to do business with AMD's Ruiz. Dell is going after more consumer business, Apple's primary turf. In late 2005, Dell introduced a higher-end XPS line, and it planned to ship Viiv PCs.

In addition, Intel executives seem open to easing their once ironclad ties to Microsoft. At the start, PC makers will have to use Microsoft's Windows Media Center Edition operating system to earn the Viiv brand—and Intel's comarketing dollars. But Intel says that this may not continue, opening the door to Viiv machines with the Linux open-source operating system or even Apple's operating system. Indeed, Kim says that he expects some PC companies to ship Viiv boxes without Windows.

Another budding relationship in Intel's march on new markets is with Google. Otellini joined the search company's board in April 2004 and has found a few areas of joint interest. For one thing, Otellini learned that Google's energy bill for its servers now exceeds the cost of the equipment. (With 100,000 servers, Google's electricity bill probably tops $50 million a year.) That prompted Otellini to explore the prospects for energy-efficient chips. In August, Intel announced that it would dump its old architecture in favor of lower-power chips in 2006.

The two companies also have a shared interest in wireless broadband. Google is exploring the possibility of setting up free Wi-Fi "hot spots" in San Francisco and other cities. Footing the bill for Net access may make sense for Google, since it would allow the company to show digital ads to any Web surfers who use the service. Intel would benefit because free Wi-Fi could increase sales of Centrino laptops. Google executives have also said that they're interested in WiMax, another wireless technology that Intel is backing. Intel plans to embed WiMax, which is similar to Wi-Fi but works over greater distances, in PC chips late in 2006.

PAY ATTENTION TO INTERNAL CHALLENGES

To bolster the push, Otellini is looking to recruit more executives from outside the company. In 2005, Maloney hired Nokia Corp. veteran Steven Gray as a key member of the cellular team. And Maloney is turning more often to Intel Vice President Sam Arditi, a cellular industry veteran with experience in radio chips and processors—key ingredients in handsets.

The result: closer ties with Nokia and Samsung, which are both collaborating with Intel on WiMax. In September 2005, Maloney also announced a deal with Research in Motion Ltd. , making it the first major name to use Intel's cellular platform of radio, processors, and memory. "The relationship is going to be very important to RIM," says co-CEO Jim Basillie.

For all that, Otellini's internal challenges may prove more daunting than the external ones. For one thing, PC chip development still casts a long shadow at the company. During Grove's and Barrett's tenures, anyone who was not producing for the core PC business was considered a second-class citizen. Barrett described the problem as akin to the creosote bush, a tall desert plant that drips poisonous oil, killing off all vegetation that tries to grow nearby. Microprocessors so dominated the company's strategy, he says, that other businesses could not sprout around it. That was one reason Otellini reorganized the company into product areas.

The shake-up hasn't helped company morale, though. Especially hard hit were the engineering teams in California and Texas, which had been working on the Pentium 4 until Otellini canceled it. Some of the design specialists have quit for new jobs, often with AMD or TI. To smooth over the problems, Otellini has toured the chipmaker's outposts, talking with engineers and others without their managers around. "A lot of what he heard was pent-up frustration, no doubt," says one engineer. "But you appreciate the fact that he's listening." Intel's attrition rate in 2005 was 4 percent, about average for the technology industry.

Sniping about the rise of marketers such as Kim continues. Says Schmuel "Mooly" Eden, an Israeli engineer who helped spearhead the Centrino launch and now heads marketing for the Mobility Group: "When I went back to Israel to talk to some of the engineers, they said: 'You're only one year in marketing, and already you're brain-damaged.'"

As Intel gears up for its big bang of product launches, there's no doubt that the mantle of leadership has shifted. This year, Otellini, for the first time, will write a performance review for Grove. In his advisory role, Grove sits in on important meetings, particularly in digital health, and gives his thoughts. Asked about the prospects of critiquing the company legend, Otellini just laughs. Reviewing Grove will be a breeze next to the challenge of remaking the world's largest chipmaker.

MONDAY MORNING...

THE PROBLEMS
Selling widespread change to employees when the company still is a market leader

Generating new, inventive products that will revolutionize the industry and also be useful to consumers

Staying on top of fast-changing trends in technology in the face of tough competition

THE SOLUTION
Articulate and explain the new mission to staff and address morale problems by listening to their concerns.

Hire outsiders who will bring new skill sets and will challenge employees to think and work differently.

Reinvigorate the culture by moving old employees into new jobs and requiring employees to team up with people with different types of expertise.

Heighten public awareness of the brand by investing in a high-profile, high-energy marketing campaign.

SUSTAINING THE WIN
Scrutinize the effectiveness of business practices and be willing to dump even age-old traditions if doing so will move the company forward.

HANS STRABERG:
ELECTROLUX CLEANS UP

© Courtesy of *BusinessWeek*.

POWER PLAYER

Since Hans Straberg became CEO of Electrolux in 2002, annual sales are on the rise and the number of product launches has almost doubled. He did it by promoting innovative R&D and launching strong cost-control measures.

This 2006 profile of Hans Straberg by Ariane Sains and Stanley Reed, with Michael Arndt, emphasizes the importance of R&D.

Expand the tools of customer research and try more innovative techniques.

Enable staff members with different expertise to collaborate by breaking down the barriers between departments.

Focus on the brand vision, creating products that not only look good but also are functional and easy to use.

Focus research and development on the needs of the consumers. Innovations are pointless unless they meet the desires of the market.

INNOVATIVE CONSUMER RESEARCH

To get a better handle on what customers want, companies need to not only pour more money into research, but be willing to do it differently. Instead of relying on traditional tools like focus groups, Electrolux now sends researchers into people's homes to observe how they actually use household products and interviews them about how these devices could be made more helpful.

You will never meet Catherine, Anna, Maria, or Monica, but the future success of Sweden's Electrolux depends on what these four women think. Catherine, for instance, a type A career woman who is a perfectionist at home, loves the idea of simply sliding her laundry basket into a washing machine instead of having to lift the clothes out of the basket and into the washer. That product idea has been moved onto the fast track for consideration.

So just who are Catherine and the other women? Well, they don't actually exist. They are composites based on in-depth interviews with some 160,000 consumers from around the globe. To divine the needs of these mythical customers, 53 Electrolux employees, including designers, engineers, and marketers hailing from various divisions, gathered in Stockholm at the end of November for a weeklong brainstorming session. The Catherine team began by ripping photographs out of a pile of magazines and sticking them onto posterboards. Next to a picture of a woman wearing a sharply tailored suit, they scribbled some of Catherine's attributes: driven, busy, and a bit overwhelmed.

With the help of these characters, Electrolux designers and engineers are searching for the insights they'll need if they are to dream up the next batch of hot products. It's a new way of doing things for Electrolux, but then again, a lot is new at the company. When Chief Executive Hans Straberg took the helm in 2002, the world's number two maker of home appliances after Whirlpool Corp. faced spiraling costs, and its middle-market products were gradually losing out to cheaper goods from Asia and Eastern Europe. Competition in the United States which is where Electrolux gets 40 percent of its sales, was ferocious. The company's stock was treading water.

SYNERGY IN ACTION

Straberg had no choice but to do something radical. He began shuttering plants in Western Europe and the United States and shifting work to lower-cost locales in Asia and Eastern Europe. He also is spinning off the outdoor products division. But this is no ordinary corporate makeover. Straberg is also breaking down barriers between departments and forcing his designers, engineers, and marketers to work together to come up with new products. To speed the transition, he has recruited executives from companies with strong track records in innovation, including Procter & Gamble and PepsiCo.

At the Stockholm brainstorming session, for example, the group leader, Kim Scott, is a recent P&G defector. She urges everyone "to think of yourselves as Catherine." The room buzzes with discussion. Ideas are refined; sketches are drawn up. The group settles on three concepts: Breeze, a clothes steamer that also removes stains; an Ironing Center, similar to a pants press but for shirts; and Ease, the washing machine that holds a laundry basket inside its drum.

Half the group races off to the machine shop to turn out a prototype for Breeze, while the rest stay upstairs to bang out a marketing plan. Over the next hour, designer Lennart Johansson carves and sandpapers a block of peach-colored polyurethane until a contraption that resembles a cross between an electric screwdriver and a handheld vacuum begins to emerge. The designers in the group want the Breeze to be smaller, but engineer Giuseppe Frucco points out that that would leave too little space for a charging station for the 1,500-watt unit.

For company veterans like Frucco, who works at Electrolux's fabric care research and development center in Porcia, Italy, this dynamic groupthink is a refreshing change: "We never used to create new products together," he says. "The designers would

To develop new products more quickly, companies need to foster teamwork across departments. Electrolux's designers, engineers, and marketers, for instance, now get together to dream up new products. The result: they are more likely to discover snafus early on, saving the company time and money.

43

When an organization wants to make big changes quickly, placing outsiders in key leadership roles can help move the process along. Straberg hired away executives with proven track records at consumer goods companies, like Procter & Gamble.

come up with something and then tell us to build it." The new way saves time and money by avoiding the technical glitches that crop up as a new design moves from the drafting table to the factory floor.

To support the innovation drive, Straberg has bumped up spending on R&D from 0.8 percent of sales to 1.2 percent and is aiming for 2 percent eventually. What he's gunning for are products that consumers will gladly pay a premium for: gadgets with drop-dead good looks and clever features that ordinary people can understand without having to pore through a thick users' manual. "Consumers are prepared to pay for good design and good performance," he says.

Electrolux isn't the only appliance maker that's on an innovation kick. In 1999, Whirlpool Corp. launched a program that allows all of its 68,000 employees to contribute design ideas, yielding a flood of new products.

EYE-CATCHING DESIGN

But few companies have pulled off the range of hot new offerings that Electrolux has. One clear hit is a cordless stick and hand vacuum, called Pronto in the United States. Available in an array of metallic hues with a rounded, ergonomic design, this is the Cinderella of vacuums. Too attractive to be locked up in the broom closet, it cries out to be displayed in your kitchen. In Europe, it now commands 50 percent of the market for stick vacuum cleaners, a coup for a product that has been on the market for fewer than two years. The Pronto is cleaning up in the United States, too. Stacy Silk, a buyer at retail chain Best Buy Co., says that it is one of her hottest sellers, even though it retails for around $100, double

The challenge for most leaders is to find ways to rein in costs without sacrificing quality. Straberg's strategy was to reduce manufacturing overhead. Seeing that inexpensive products were gradually elbowing out Electrolux's mid-range products, Straberg closed down plants in Western Europe and the United States and shifted the work to Asia and Eastern Europe.

the price of comparable models. "The biggest thing is the aesthetics," Silk says. "That gets people to walk over and look."

Straberg, who spent decades running Electrolux operations in the United States, is crafting these new products while at the same time moving away from many traditional tools of customer research. The company is relying less heavily on focus groups; it now prefers to interview people in their homes, where they can be videotaped pushing a vacuum or shoving laundry into the washer. "Consumers think they know what they want, but they often have trouble articulating it," says Henrik Otto, senior vice president for global design, whom Straberg lured away from automaker Volvo. "But when we watch them, we can ask, 'Why do you do that?' We can change the product and solve their problems."

The new approach is starting to yield results. After dropping for two straight years, annual sales rose 8 percent, to $16.5 billion, in 2005. Operating income jumped 42 percent in the fourth quarter of 2005, compared with the year before, though it rose by less than 2 percent, to $881 million, for the year as a whole. Johan Hjertonsson, director of the consumer innovation program, says that product launches have almost doubled in quantity. And the number of launches that result in outsized unit sales is now running at 50 percent of all introductions, from around 25 percent previously. The stock? Up a third in the last year. Catherine would be pleased.

Companies that value creativity and ingenuity understand that ideas need not come only from the top. Whirlpool, the world's largest maker of home appliances, encourages all of its 68,000 employees to contribute design ideas.

MONDAY MORNING...

THE PROBLEM

Achieving growth at a time when costs are escalating and competitors are chipping away at the company's sales

Finding a way to develop top-notch products that customers are willing to pay a premium for

THE STRATEGY

Take actions that will reduce spending without hindering the organization's long-term objective of developing top-notch goods.

Champion new, more effective ways of conducting consumer research.

Bring together employees with different skill sets for brainstorming sessions.

SUSTAINING THE WIN

Maintain the emphasis on inventiveness and quality so that the company continues to reach its goals.

THE ALBRECHT BROTHERS: ALDI AND TRADER JOE'S CHALLENGE TO WAL-MART

Karl Albrecht

©Wirtschaftswoche

Theo Albrecht

©Wirtschaftswoche

Reject the bigger-is-better philosophy and keep costs low by selling fewer items.

Find ways to reduce expenses in all areas, from the products that the company stocks to where it is located.

Maintain control over quality by selling primarily store brands.

POWER PLAYER

In the era of the superstore, Karl and Theo Albrecht are pursuing a counterintuitive strategy by offering limited selections at deep discounts.

This chapter combines 2004 cover story on Aldi by Jack Ewing with a story on Trader Joe's by Larry Armstrong.

MORE IS NOT ALWAYS BETTER

The Albrecht brothers' strategy is carried out in both their U.S.-based specialty food chain and their German-based grocery stores. Taking the empire worldwide, Aldi is one of the largest grocers in the world.

At first glance, an Aldi Group store in Germany seems like an unlikely staging area for world conquest. Jars of asparagus and cans of sardines poke out of cardboard boxes piled on pallets. The line at the registers is 10 people long, and the product range is reminiscent of East Berlin, circa 1975. Two brands of toilet paper. One brand of pickles. But the prices are delightfully, breathtakingly low. Three frozen pizzas for $3.24. A bottle of decent Cabernet: $2.36. How about a $21 trench coat?

Germany may be the land of the $100,000 Mercedes-Benz land yacht, but it's also a land of ebbing wealth, where less than a fifth of the population has discretionary income of more than $375 a month, where even the *haut bourgeois* will lay out for a fancy car but stint on the staples. Thus, Aldi stores are found not only in working-class neighborhoods, but also in wealthy communities like Bad Homburg, a Frankfurt suburb, where the Aldi parking lot is thick with BMWs and Mercedes. A cookbook devoted to recipes using Aldi ingredients has sold 1 million copies, and there is even a connoisseur's guide to Aldi wines, which often sell for a few dollars a bottle. A recent survey by Nuremberg-based market researcher GfK found that Aldi is Germany's third-most-respected corporate brand, just behind electronics giant Siemens and automaker BMW—and ahead of DaimlerChrysler.

An astonishing 89 percent of German households shopped at Aldi at least once last year, according to GfK. That has made the company's reclusive cofounder Karl Albrecht the world's third-richest man, with a fortune estimated at $23 billion by *Forbes* magazine. Aldi—short for "Albrecht Discount"—"is a huge cult," says Matthias Kövér, a Cologne resident who maintains a Web site for devotees.

POWER MOVE

The Albrecht brothers understand that customers will give up choice in exchange for savings. Although a typical grocer sells 20,000 products, Aldi stores sell just 700 bargain-priced basics. Keeping inventory low helps Aldi keep shipping and handling costs down, which, in turn, keeps prices low.

LESS CHOICE WITH MORE SAVINGS

Aldi is Europe's stealth Wal-Mart. Like the Arkansas-based giant, Aldi boasts awesome margins, huge market clout, and seemingly unstoppable growth—including an estimated sales increase of 8 percent a year since 1998. It relentlessly focuses on efficiency, matching or even beating Wal-Mart Stores Inc. in its ability to strip out costs. Yet privately owned Aldi is also very old-school German, financing its expansion with cash to avoid debt, shunning publicity, and moving quietly into new markets before the competition catches on. That has allowed the onetime local grocer in Essen to become one of the world's biggest retailers, with $37 billion in sales, a fraction of Wal-Mart's $245 billion but enough to give Aldi a 3.5 percent market share in Europe, vs. 6.8 percent for market leader Carrefour, according to Brussels-based market watcher M+M Planet Retail. Even mighty Wal-Mart has struggled against Aldi in Germany. Wal-Mart has other problems there, such as a lack of sites for its jumbo-size stores. But a big obstacle is that Aldi and other discounters already have a lock on budget food shoppers. "Aldi was doing the same thing as Wal-Mart before Wal-Mart got here," says Frank Pietersen, a retail analyst for KPMG in Cologne.

The discount chain already is having a Wal-Mart-type effect on the German economy. The main association of German retailers issued a report on March 8 blaming Aldi and other "hard discounters" for running 35,000 small shops out of business last year. On the same day, Bavarian dairy farmers picketed Aldi stores, which they blame for a ruinous 15 percent plunge in milk prices since 2001. Aldi must take care not to let such criticism tarnish its reputation among German consumers.

What's next? Aldi now shows signs of stepping up the pace of its expansion on Wal-Mart's turf. Aldi opened its first U.S. store in Iowa in 1976 and has sales of $4.8 billion in North America, according to M+M. And Trader Joe's Co., a specialty grocer owned by a family trust that Aldi cofounder Theo Albrecht created for his sons, has become the hottest thing in U.S. retailing by extending the Aldi concept to upscale products like wine and cashew butter.

POWER MOVE

Both Trader Joe's and Aldi have found success by not stocking name brands, but developing and selling primarily their own products instead. That allows the two chains to maintain quality control and offer lower prices.

DON'T RUSH—DO RESEARCH FIRST

Aldi aims to open 40 stores a year until 2010, bringing the U.S. total to 1,000. Aldi is even buying up sites from retailers that have been trampled by Wal-Mart. "It is an uncharacteristic weakness of Wal-Mart that it has not recognized how formidable a foe Aldi is," warns Burt P. Flickinger III of New York City–based Strategic Resource Group, a retailing and consumer goods consultant. He expects Aldi to have as much as 2 percent of the U.S. grocery market by the end of the decade, up from 0.65 percent now. Says Wal-Mart spokesman Bill Wertz: "We certainly recognize Aldi as being a tough competitor."

Will Aldi take over the world? It's clear that it is on the march, advertising on the Web for workers and store locations in places such as Ireland and Australia. "One of the principles of Aldi is not to rush into things, but first to build a solid foundation. Once they have that, they move more quickly," says Dieter Brandes, a former Aldi executive who has published a book, *The 11 Secrets of Aldi Success.*

Aldi—actually two associated retailing groups controlled by Karl Albrecht and his brother Theo, both in their 80s—is Europe's biggest "hard discounter," the term for a retailer that pushes prices even lower than traditional discounters. Hard discounters have doubled their share of the European grocery market in the past decade, to 9.5 percent, according to ACNielsen. "They're coming, and they're going to change the retailing landscape for good," says Volker Koch, Frankfurt-based analyst for M+M.

Aldi follows a simple but devastating strategy. A typical Aldi store has only about 700 products, compared with more than 20,000 at a traditional grocer such as Royal Ahold's Albert Heijn and as many as 150,000 at a Wal-Mart Supercenter. Established brand names like Nestlé or Nivea or Persil are irrelevant at Aldi. Almost everything on display is an Aldi-exclusive label, such as Frisco Dent toothpaste (61 cents for a family-size tube) or Rio D'Oro orange juice (74 cents a liter) in Europe. The Aldi lineup even seems to be winning over U.S. shoppers. "They're not

> Any company that is bent on expansion faces the distinct danger of overextending itself. The Albrechts minimize the risks by financing new stores with cash and moving stealthily into new markets. Avoiding publicity has enabled the stores to get established before their rivals take notice.

the brands I'm used to, but they're good. Nestlé has nothing on this," says retired schoolteacher Silvia Randall, holding up a package of LaMissa hot cocoa mix at an Aldi in Smyrna, Georgia.

SIMPLICITY MATTERS

Because it sells so few products, Aldi can exert strong control over quality and price. The limited selection simplifies shipping and handling. A survey by consultants McKinsey & Co. found that shoppers perceived little difference in quality, assortment, or service at Aldi vs. traditional retailers, but they rated Aldi better on price. "We have a lot of respect for Aldi quality," says Wolfgang Gutberlet, CEO of Fulda, Germany–based tegut, which operates about 300 food stores in western Germany.

FOCUS ON QUALITY AT THE LOWEST PRICE

The fanatic attention to costs pays off. Aldi's operating margin in some regions of Germany is as high as 9.3 percent, according to McKinsey. "Aldi has taken the retail formula down to the most basic elements," says Neil Z. Stern, senior partner at Chicago retail consultant McMillan/ Doolittle LLP, who believes that Aldi is more efficient than Wal-Mart. One knowledgeable estimate puts pretax profits at $1.5 billion.

Like all greater marketers, the Albrecht brothers understand their customers. While Aldi's caters to bargain hunters, Trader Joe's appeals to shoppers with upscale tastes. So TJ products don't include genetically modified ingredients, and even its peanut butter is organic.

Aldi's formula is as much the result of necessity as of brilliance. When Karl and Theo Albrecht returned from Allied POW camps after World War II, residents of bombed-out Essen wanted only the products they needed from one day to the next, for the best price. So the brothers restricted their assortment to a few hundred items and monitored quality carefully. "Our business was managed solely on the basis of the lowest price," Karl Albrecht said during a rare public appearance in 1975. The Albrechts have avoided the spotlight since 1971, when Theo was kidnapped for 17 days. He was released in return for a $4 million ransom—after bargaining to get the price down, according to press reports.

Frugality remains an obsession. Theo Albrecht turns off lights when he enters a room if he thinks daylight suffices, according to Brandes. Theo still goes to work each day, while Karl has turned over day-to-day management to professionals. Brandes says that little is likely to change when the Albrechts are gone: ownership has been transferred to trusts to avoid disputes among heirs.

Will Aldi prove as successful a German export as BMWs? In Europe, retailers are certainly feeling the heat. The Netherlands Albert Heijn cut prices on 2,000 products last year to try to thwart the hard discounters. ACNielsen even sells a risk assessment profile to help other retailers figure out when an Aldi product threatens their sales. However, foreign grocers have had lots of time to prepare for Aldi. In Britain, Aldi has just 1 percent of the grocery market 14 years after opening its first store. Tesco PLC has defended its share with its own low-priced brands. Hard discounter Lidl, a unit of Neckarsulm-based Lidl & Schwarz Group, leads Aldi in France and Britain and is moving into Eastern Europe, where Aldi so far is absent. "I think they'll be challenged to extend their footprint any farther," says Richard Hull, who heads the retail team at London consultants Cap Gemini Ernst & Young Group.

ALL-CASH APPROACH TO EXPANSION

Aldi's all-cash approach to expansion means that its risk is low. Analysts say that Aldi could find a niche in U.S. markets that can't support a "big box" store such as Costco Wholesale Corp. And most U.S. retailers don't seem to recognize the threat. "[Aldi] is kind of bottom-feeding, and nobody notices it," says Tom A. Muccio, a former Procter & Gamble Co. executive. Funny, that's the same mistake that German competitors made a few decades ago.

TRADER JOE'S: THE TRENDY AMERICAN COUSIN

It's a small grocery chain that moves into abandoned retail stores in second-rate locations. Parking is all but impossible. There's not a deep selection in the cramped aisles, and you'll be lucky to spot a national brand on the shelves.

Welcome to Trader Joe's. About all that this 210-store U.S. chain has in common with Germany's Aldi Group—besides being owned by a trust created by Aldi cofounder Theo Albrecht—is its rigorous control over costs. But where Aldi carries such basics as toilet paper and canned peas, TJ's, as it's known, stocks eclectic and upscale foodstuffs for the wine-and-cheese set at down-to-earth prices.

It's a phenomenally lucrative combination, analysts say. Sales last year were an estimated $2.1 billion, or $1,132 per square foot, twice those of traditional supermarkets, according to the Food Institute, a nonprofit research group in Elmwood Park, New Jersey. The Monrovia, California, company would not talk to *BusinessWeek*, but its Web site notes that while the 37-year-old chain quintupled its store count from 1990 to 2001, profits grew tenfold.

UNIQUE FEEL-GOOD SELECTION AT FEEL-GOOD PRICES

"What's unique about Trader Joe's is that there's no competition," says Willard R. Bishop Jr., who heads his own consulting firm in Barrington, Illinois. TJ's develops or imports many of its own products from sources it has developed over decades and sells more than 80 percent of them under the Trader Joe's brand or a variant thereof: Trader José, Trader Ming, and Baker Josef are a few. In states where it can, it sells discount wine and liquor. The latest rage is its own Charles Shaw label of California varietals, affectionately known as Two-Buck Chuck for its $1.99 price tag in California (it's $3.39 in Ohio stores).

Famously frugal, the Albrechts are known for leading very lean, efficient organizations. To cut costs, Trader Joe's often puts its stores in abandoned retail space in second-rate locations, while the Aldi chain has small staffs and nonunion workers.

It's not all about value pricing. Trader Joe's products have a definite feel-good bent. The company promises that products with the TJ label won't include genetically modified ingredients. After complaints from animal-rights activists about the way ducks are slaughtered, it stopped selling them. Ahi tuna is caught without nets, dried apricots are unsulfured, the peanut butter is organic—and has no trans fats to boot. And what about those Ghirardelli chocolate-covered dried blueberries, $3.99 for a 10-oz tub? TJ's notes that you can get your choco-fix and your antioxidants at the same time.

One place where TJ's has never stinted is with its employees. Besides above-union wages and generous bonuses (pay for entry-level part-timers starts at $8 to $12 an hour; first-year supervisors average more than $40,000 a year), TJ's contributes an additional 15.4 percent of each worker's gross pay to a company-funded retirement plan.

The company got its start in the 1960s, when Joe Coulombe was trying to figure out how to protect his three southern California convenience stores, called Pronto Markets, from the onslaught of 7-Elevens. He loaded up the stores with hard-to-find gourmet items and low-priced wines, and cherry-picked food manufacturers' discontinued and overstocked merchandise, which he peddled at steep discounts. Coulombe sold the renamed Trader Joe's in 1979 to the family trust established by Theo Albrecht, and he retired in 1988.

The ever-changing closeouts turned shopping at TJ's into something of a treasure hunt. The closeouts are now mostly gone, but with its wide selection of unique products and a friendly staff (they're the ones in the funky Hawaiian shirts), it remains that today. For most people, shopping is a chore. Trader Joe's makes it recreation.

THE PROBLEM

Selling high-quality goods at prices lower than even the discounters

Pursuing new markets and maintaining aggressive growth while also continuing to scrupulously manage finances

THE SOLUTION

Cut costs by limiting inventory, forgoing name brands, and selling primarily company-branded goods.

Keep overhead low by opening stores in middling locations.

Take a cautious approach to expansion, using cash to pay for new stores and adding new ones when others are well established.

SUSTAINING THE WIN

Keep an almost fanatical attention on the bottom line, cutting costs, but without sacrificing the quality that consumers have come to expect.

ANNE LIVERMORE:
HP'S ULTIMATE TEAM PLAYER

©John Abbott

POWER PLAYER

When Anne Livermore took the helm of HP's troubled Technology Solutions Group, she saw an exciting opportunity where others saw a certain failure. She realized that the market could be segmented differently, allowing her to focus on different customers and to devise products and services that would make their lives easier.

Peter Burrows' profile from early 2006 looks at how Anne Livermore has helped revive Hewlett-Packard.

Institute change in a company that has a strong culture.

Identify a need and seize the opportunity to address and fill it.

Formulate a vision for success and develop a plan to achieve it.

Refocus efforts on a new customer segment that presents different, challenging needs.

Take advantage of a long history of doing things "the HP way".

Engineer a turnaround in the face of senior management turmoil.

Show commitment to changes in management in order to create a unified team.

THE LURE OF OPPORTUNITY

One of Livermore's most important traits is her ability to formulate a vision for success, develop a plan to achieve it, and inspire others to join her for the ride. Livermore, found a way to maintain and convey her enthusiasm for the company and its exciting opportunities.

One July evening in Silicon Valley, Hewlett-Packard Co. (HPQ) executive Anne Livermore got the phone call she had waited months to receive. She rushed to the hospital, having learned that a kidney had been donated, and underwent an organ transplant, necessary due to complications from a childhood disease. For most executives, it would have been an opportune time to call it quits after a 24-year career. But three days after the surgery, she was phoning HP Chief Executive Mark V. Hurd and peppering lieutenants with questions. "I finally asked if someone would please go in there and take her laptop away," laughs Hurd.

Why didn't Livermore step down? Opportunity. While the $33 billion corporate-computing business she runs has long been one of the most glaring underachievers in tech, she's convinced the business is finally ready to show what it can do. Livermore and HP have spent 18 months overhauling the unit, and the benefits are only now becoming visible. "From the moment I left, I never thought of not coming back," says Livermore, who was out for 5$1/2$ weeks. "We have a very special opportunity right now."

THE TURNAROUND

It's a dramatic reversal. A year previously her Technology Solutions Group, which sells servers, storage, and consulting services to corporations, was valued at next to nothing by Wall Street analysts. Mercilessly squeezed by IBM (IBM) and Dell Inc. (DELL), the unit struggled to show profits or promise. Indeed, while HP's printer business brought in nearly all of the company's earnings, Livermore's unit became a millstone around the neck of former CEO Carleton S. Fiorina, contributing to her ouster a year ago.

Yet Livermore's unit is now a key reason HP's stock is on a tear, and the newly arrived Hurd is being hailed as a turnaround maestro. Thanks mostly to cost cutting and operational improvements, the businesses turned in a 50 percent increase in operating earnings in fiscal 2005, to $1.9 billion, on revenues of $33.2 billion. Overall, HP earned $4.2 billion for the year, on revenues of $86.7 billion.

Now, rather than bemoaning how bad the corporate business is, analysts are trying to figure out how good it can be. What was once rated an F has become a C business. Can Livermore bring the grade up to a B or even an A? It's an open question, though there's little doubt the next phase will be harder than the last. "They're certainly doing better," says Richard E. Belluzzo, a longtime HP exec who now heads the storage company Quantum Corp. "They've done some good work, particularly on the cost side. But the strategic challenges are pretty much the same."

Harsh perhaps, but true. While HP wants its corporate unit to be a leaner, meaner alternative to IBM, it remains far behind Big Blue in several key areas, including high-end computing, software, and such services as consulting and outsourcing. In software, for example, HP's revenues are about $1 billion, compared with IBM's $16 billion. And other rivals expect HP to grow complacent, given its recent improvements. "I'm happy they're feeling happy about their success, because it means they'll get apathetic—and we'll clean their clocks," says Daniel J. Warmenhoven, another former HP executive who now runs storage highflier Network Appliance Inc.

POSITIONED FOR GROWTH

Yet HP is better positioned than in the past. For starters, Hurd has brought the company's costs in line by laying off about 15,000 employees, or 10 percent of its workforce. It also has a stronger product lineup, particularly in storage and software, where HP has made nine acquisitions in 18 months. Just as important, Hurd and Livermore are beginning to articulate a strategy for corporate customers that's truly distinct from IBM's, not just a similar approach with a different name.

The difference? While IBM leads with its consulting services and its ability to help

Hurd and Livermore understand the need for broad, decisive action. With massive layoffs, numerous acquisitions, and significant product mix changes, the two have their hands full. However, both leaders know that this isn't yet the time to relax.

the top brass devise corporate strategy, HP is focused on helping companies get a handle on the soaring costs of maintaining and powering their tech gear. The goal is to use software and other automation technologies to reduce the number of tech staffers by 90 percent, at the same time they slash the amount of energy tech equipment uses. Livermore's ideal is a "lights out" data center, with almost no human involvement. While IBM goes after chief executives, HP is tailoring its message for chief information officers, the people who oversee corporate technology. "We're focused on addressing CIOs' biggest pain point," says Livermore. "Customers are complaining that all their money goes into labor and operating costs. We can be the company to help them automate and manage this, to drive costs out."

In many ways, Livermore is a perfect metaphor for HP. The 46-year-old is competent, respected, but not really feared by rivals. A standout tennis player and valedictorian of her high school in Greensboro, N.C., she earned a coveted Morehouse Scholarship to the University of North Carolina at Chapel Hill. She went straight to business school at Stanford University. There, she won the annual competition for best business plan for running the doughnut concession. Her secret? She solicited companies that were coming to interview students to buy her sweets by the dozen.

When she joined HP, straight out of Stanford, she never expected to make a career of it. She had watched her father stay at the same insurance company for years and vowed not to get bogged down. But she fell in love with HP's unique culture. Especially appealing was HP's willingness to accommodate working mothers through flexible working hours and other arrangements. Livermore could dote on her daughter, even as she roared through the ranks. By 1996 she was running the services arm. In 1999, she made a very public run at the CEO job—even hiring an internal

> Undoubtedly, the competition between Livermore and Fiorina was intense. However, after the battle ended, and Fiorina was declared the victor, Livermore didn't just play along, but showed her commitment to the company and to its new leader. Senior leaders need to function as a competent, cohesive team, united by their vision for success.

press relations person to raise her profile. She lost out to Fiorina and then became a staunch ally.

INAUSPICIOUS START

For all her success, Livermore still has something to prove. Wall Streeters are wary of her ability to deliver consistent financial results. Even some HP insiders ascribe her rise to a selfless willingness to follow orders. They're quick to point out that she's a solid general manager and universally well-liked but question whether she can rally the troops to challenge a fierce foe like IBM. "She's extremely competent," says one insider, "but I don't see her as a key leader for the long-term." Completing the turnaround in the corporate business could help Livermore win over the naysayers. She may even get another shot at the chief executive job, although Hurd, at 49, likely will hold the post for a good number of years.

Livermore had an inauspicious start in her current job. She took over the corporate computing business in early 2004. Just three months later, in August, it reported a disastrous quarter, causing HP to miss its earnings estimates by 33 percent and pushing the company's stock down 15 percent.

Out of that crisis, Livermore has helped forge a comeback. Within days, she instructed HP veteran Scott Stallard to set up a war room to begin addressing the unit's many operational problems. Over the months that followed, she worked closely with a seven-person team to identify and improve 15 key weaknesses—everything from how HP worked with distributors to how it pulled together bids for customers. One accomplishment: HP established an Integrated Bid Desk that reduced the time it took to generate prices for complex corporate deals from two weeks to one day.

The improvements couldn't save Fiorina, though. She was pushed out in early February of last year.

In times of crisis, establishing a central hub of activity, like HP's "war room," can increase an organization's focus, set a healthy level of urgency, and imbue team members with a deep sense of purpose. HP showed its willingness to solving the business unit's toughest issues. Despite the debacle of her first three months, Livermore didn't give up. She doubled down and showed her commitment to capturing the enormous opportunity before her.

ON THE MOVE

As the company searched for a new chief, Livermore headed out to talk with customers. In March she visited four large Wall Street firms and was struck by the problems these big tech buyers were suffering from. "Every one of the CIOs was complaining that while their spending on tech equipment was declining, their spending on operations— mostly labor—was increasing an average of 10 percent per year. They were pleading for ways to automate more," says Livermore. "They all believed HP was a company that could help them."

From New York, Livermore traveled to Phoenix, where 80 of HP's top researchers had gathered for an annual technology confab. At the gathering, which is structured like a trade show with demonstration booths, Livermore saw a series of technologies that could help the CIOs she had just met on Wall Street. She pow-wowed with Shane Robison, HP's chief technologist, and his staff. Together, they hatched a plan centered on creating the "next-generation data center."

From the start, Livermore knew that she had to find a way to differentiate HP from its powerful competitors. She used an age-old marketing technique: figure out what you do best, and find the customers that want it. By going directly to her customers, Livermore heard loud and clear what CIOs worry about most. She connected the dots to how HP could help them, consulted with the technology experts who could help develop her plan, and then moved quickly to execute.

Hurd came on board later that month, on March 29. In their first meetings, Livermore urged him to slash HP's cost structure, to boost profits and clean out bureaucracy. She also encouraged Hurd to improve HP's sales effort by investing in software tools to help salesmen analyze deals more quickly and promoting sales vets to run more of HP's businesses.

In all these cases, she got her wish. In July, Hurd laid off thousands and gave Livermore and her fellow division chiefs more control over their respective sales and marketing efforts. Soon after, she accelerated plans to hire more storage and server salespeople and implemented a new compensation plan to boost sales of software, including the next-generation data center technologies. The once-insular HP is also hiring and promoting outsiders to fill key posts. Among others, Steve Smith, a hard-driving former Electronic Data

> In a turnaround situation, leaders have to move fast. Decisive action helps preempt the complaints of detractors and critics and instills confidence in nervous employees: the new leaders have a vision and are moving quickly to achieve it.

Systems Corp. (EDS) salesman, now runs the $15 billion services business.

BLOWING HP'S HORN

The payoff came in November, when HP showed investors surprisingly strong results. The corporate computing business was the real shocker, with the storage and server unit posting operating earnings of $405 million, about four times the total a year earlier.

By December, the normally hype-free Hurd was ready to crow a bit. At a packed meeting of financial analysts in Manhattan, he said Livermore's division would lead the way toward a "lights-out" data center. "If you look at our raw technology, I don't think there's another company in the world that has a lead on HP," he said.

A growing number of analysts think Livermore's business is back on solid footing. Merrill Lynch & Co. analyst Richard Farmer predicts the unit will see operating profits rise another 50 percent this year, to $3 billion, while revenues increase to $35.1 billion.

But can HP become a leader on par with IBM, setting the trends in technology? That's a separate question. "They're in the process of turning it around, but I wouldn't hand them the keys to the kingdom just yet," says Goldman Sachs & Co. analyst Laura Conigliaro.

Livermore recognizes that both she and HP have their doubters. But she believes time is on their side. "The fact is, there's no one better in the world at helping customers design, build, and manage data centers," she says. "We have not proudly or loudly enough put that stake in the ground. But we will." The company's future—and her own—may depend on it.

> Like all good marketers, Livermore is consistently on message. By continuing to emphasize HP's new strategy, she conveys a strong sense of focus.

MONDAY MORNING...

MONDAY

THE PROBLEMS

Turning around an ailing business unit in the face of fierce, powerful competition

Finding a way to distinguish your business from the rest of the pack, without simply following the leaders

Leading with confidence while the future of the company is uncertain

THE SOLUTION

Find the customers that other firms are ignoring and listen for business problems that are common to many of them.

Collaborate with experts who can help you develop a winning plan.

Equip managers with the tools and authority to make changes in their divisions.

SUSTAINING THE WIN

Move quickly to show competitors, employees, customers, and investors that you are committed to achieving success.

HARLAN WEISMAN
REINVENTING HOW
JOHNSON & JOHNSON INVENTS

©Richard Freeda / Aurora

POWER PLAYER

With J & J's earnings growth poised to fall and its stock price suffering, Chief Science and Technology Officer Harlan Weisman is leading an aggressive effort to develop more top-notch products. His strategy: encouraging collaboration and nurturing the smart ideas.

This April 2006 story by Amy Barrett looks at J&J as it bets on a new push for product development as a cure for its ailing stock.

Cultivate cutting-edge ideas by creating an entrepreneurial culture, encouraging employees to come up with exciting new business initiatives.

Promote cooperation between departments so that the organization better uses the skills and knowledge of its workers.

Identify new market opportunities by looking in the "white spaces," the areas that others might have overlooked.

UNUSUAL PLACES FOR INSPIRATION

These days, managers at Johnson & Johnson are willing to look in some unusual places for inspiration. In 2005, a small unit within Johnson & Johnson's Ethicon Endo-Surgery tools business was brainstorming about how to design a better surgical clip. A team consisting of seven scientists and engineers fanned out to buy as many clips of any type as they could find. They grabbed a motley collection—more than 100 of them—from Wal-Mart Stores, Home Depot, and other local hardware and hobby shops. Those clips now hang on a big board in the group's warehouselike research and development offices outside Cincinnati. "The idea was to free [the team] up," says Dr. Harlan Weisman, chief science and technology officer for Johnson & Johnson's device and diagnostic unit. "Let them be like kids and maybe they'll come up with a nifty solution."

The shopping spree is just one small example of how the 120-year-old company is trying to drive innovation in its growing, increasingly important medical device business. Johnson & Johnson executives are trying to replicate the fertile and fast-moving venture-capital world, creating internal start-ups that hunt for financing among other J&J units as they would if they were independent.

Johnson & Johnson is also pushing for greater input from doctors and insurers to guarantee that it knows exactly what devices customers will want—and what sort of data they will demand before using those devices. The company is even tinkering with its much-vaunted decentralized management structure, putting Weisman in his newly created position in 2005 as a way to bring greater focus to the task of identifying new markets. "It's not your father's Johnson & Johnson," Weisman asserts.

> Even the blue chips have to be willing to reevaluate their traditions. J&J recognized that it could create more breakthrough devices if there were more synergy between its various units. So J&J put Dr. Harlan Weisman in his new position.

COLLABORATION IS KEY

There's a sense of urgency at the New Brunswick, New Jersey, icon. With $16 billion in cash, J&J is on the prowl for sizable acquisitions. But after being outbid for Guidant Corp. earlier this year, it knows all too well that potential targets won't come cheap. Without a shot in the arm in the form of new products, however, earnings growth is expected to make a major downshift. While earnings per share were up an average of 16.2 percent annually over the past five years, Morgan Stanley (MS) analyst Glenn Reicin expects them to grow an average of just 8.4 percent for each of the next five years. It's no surprise, then, that Wall Street has been backing away from the company's stock, which fell 13 percent in the past year, to $59 on April 4,2006. Once a premium stock, J&J is now occasionally the subject of breakup speculation.

Like many corporate giants, J&J has relied heavily on acquisitions to fuel its growth. In a bid to innovate, managers with a great idea and a solid business plan can get funding from J&J's venture-capital unit.

The health-care giant's record of internal innovation simply hasn't kept pace with its increasingly massive size. The challenges are particularly worrisome in J&J's $19 billion devices and diagnostics business, which represents 38 percent of overall revenues. Last year that unit fueled the company's growth as its big drug operation slowed. And J&J Chairman and CEO William C. Weldon made it clear with his ill-fated Guidant bid that he wanted to shift the business mix away from pharmaceuticals, where the entire industry pipeline is weak, and toward devices.

That's why Weisman's new job is so critical. A rising star at J&J, Weisman, 53, came to the company in 1999 with the acquisition of biotech company Centocor Inc. That deal, which brought J&J the blockbuster rheumatoid arthritis drug Remicade, was seen as a home run. After years on the pharmaceutical side, Weisman is now charged not only with identifying key new markets for J&J to go after in devices but also with spotting ways in which the drug and device businesses might collaborate to create new products.

Weisman's cross-functional appointment—a device guy with a pharmaceutical past—underscores a subtle cultural shift. J&J has long cultivated a decentralized organization, allowing more than 200 companies to operate almost as autonomous businesses.

As useful as that is for a prolific acquirer, it may not be the ideal structure for spotting new markets. And while J&J managers have often spoken about the potential offered by combining devices and drugs in one product, the company's decentralization can also create barriers to that sort of synergy. Asking managers suddenly to change the basic way they operate and collaborate "to some extent is countercultural," says Michael L. Tushman, a professor of business administration at Harvard Business School.

SPOTTING OPPORTUNITIES IN THE "WHITE SPACES"

Having cross-functional skills is a major asset for Weisman, and he is better able to break down the barriers and foster communication among scientists, engineers, marketers, and others in J&J's diverse units.

Part of Weisman's new responsibility is to coax that process along. He's charged with helping to spot opportunities in what he calls "white spaces," markets that any one of J&J's existing business units might miss. He will also try to foster cooperation among various J&J units as the worlds of devices, drugs, and diagnostics converge. J&J has had some notable successes there, the most obvious being its $2.6 billion drug-coated Cypher stent. As more of those possibilities arise, Weisman will be central to getting the disparate groups to work together.

Some notable failures make it clear why the rethinking of innovation is critical. J&J's Charite artificial spinal disk was a flop, as a lack of long-term safety data led Medicare to resist covering it. Now J&J is emphasizing projects that produce more cost-effective solutions to health-care problems, with more input from end users. For example, the Ethicon-Endo unit that is designing the new surgical clip grew out of discussions with physicians about the need to find ways to do less-invasive surgeries. In 2001, the business carved out a new, skunk-works-like unit made up not only of scientists and engineers, but also of marketing and regulatory experts who understand what payers will want. The group moved into its own facility five miles down the road from the Ethicon-Endo business, and it was given what Nick Valeriani, J&J's worldwide chairman of cardiovascular devices and diagnostics, calls a "bucketful of money" to create new surgical tools.

ENTREPRENEURIAL CULTURE

J&J is trying to spark the creation of more of those start-ups. Two years ago, the company began encouraging managers with ideas for cutting-edge new businesses to shop for funding within the company. Teams with a hot idea create a business plan and try to win financing from the company's big venture-capital arm, known as Johnson & Johnson Development Corp.,

Finding truly great ideas requires a willingness to look in unlikely places. Weisman encourages teams to have freewheeling brainstorming sessions.

and from one or more of J&J's existing businesses. JJDC has seeded outside start-ups for years, often taking stakes in companies that J&J would later buy outright. Now the idea is to put some of that VC money to work within the company itself. Already, Weisman claims, the effort has yielded four new projects, including one researching adult stem cells.

While Wall Street is clearly worried about a slowdown in the device business, J&J executives argue that the company has not stumbled. Weisman says that the rethinking of J&J's new-product development reflects the shift in the world of medical devices to even more complex products, rather than evidence of any slipup on J&J's part. "I was not brought in to fix something that was broken," Weisman insists. It's true that J&J's R&D operation, with about 15,000 people worldwide, has enjoyed its fair share of breakthroughs. And J&J keeps that R&D machine well greased, having spent $6.3 billion on it last year.

But for a company with a $176 billion market cap, it's going to be tough to find new ventures that will move the needle. Shifting away from the traditional R&D approach toward a more integrated, cross-disciplinary approach to innovation is a start. J&J, one of the bluest of the blue chips, needs to have something happen fairly soon to recharge its growth and rejuvenate its sagging share price. J&J's problems are significant, but Weisman's business philosophy is pretty simple. "If it works," he says, "we'll keep doing it."

MONDAY MORNING...

THE PROBLEM
Creating more innovative products that will be embraced by the marketplace

Finding ways to spark more inventive business ideas

THE STRATEGY
Emphasize team building across divisions so that the organization leverages the strengths and knowledge of its workers.

Increase the odds that a new device will be successful by soliciting feedback from end users—doctors, insurers, and others—during product development.

Leverage the strengths of employees in the different businesses by encouraging them to work together.

Make sure that the leader has the cross-functional skills to communicate with different groups.

SUSTAINING THE WIN
Make sure to analyze every aspect of the culture and be willing to change even a long-established business practice if it is hindering creativity.

JUDY McGRATH:
KEEPING MTV COOL

©Brad Trent

Judy McGrath transformed MTV Networks from a scrappy upstart into a $17 billion behemoth by embracing edgy programming and nurturing talent. Now, she is trying to keep the organization on top by expanding it to new ventures and platforms.

This February 2006 story by Tom Lowry examines how CEO Judy McGrath must remake her TV empire for a digital world.

Create a culture that values diversity and listens to ideas from all corners of the organization. Take on risky, groundbreaking projects that will make a big splash with audiences, even if that might provoke controversy.

Recognize and trust the talent, giving people the space to be creative and follow their vision. Use research as a tool for creativity. Focus groups don't have to kill the creative spark. Feed creatives the information, and let them make something out of it.

Make change part of your DNA. Don't take success for granted, and continually "reapply" to retain your success to stay sharp.

LISTEN AND LEARN

Nearly 40 years ago, in a blue-collar Irish neighborhood in Scranton, Pennsylvania, Judy McGrath fell in love with music. While her father, Charles, tried to get his only child to listen to Duke Ellington on the family hi-fi, she preferred the Rolling Stones and, later, Neil Young. Her mother, Ann, read *The Catcher in the Rye* to her when she was seven and explained to Judy that the nuns at her Catholic grade school weren't always right; she could have an opinion, too.

It was in this progressive environment in the McGraths' small house on Orchard Street that Judy began to imagine a life beyond Scranton, in New York. "It felt like a land far, far away," she recalls. "I'd never been to New York City until I came here looking for a job. It felt impossible, like there was a sense of a tribe of people I wanted to be part of. So I had this idea that I could write about music. That would be the ideal job for me." She eventually set her sights on *Rolling Stone*, that pinnacle of pop culture in the late 1960s.

McGrath made it to New York, but she never got to work at her favorite magazine. Instead, her life took a magical detour that led her to write on-air promotions for a new invention, music television.

Twenty-five years later, at 53, she is chair and CEO of MTV Networks Co. The $7 billion a year operation that she oversees is a collection of some of the most recognizable brands in the business, from the original MTV to Nickelodeon to VH1 to Comedy Central. Their programs are seen in 169 countries and heard in 28 languages. Under her management are such youth icons as SpongeBob SquarePants, the *South Park* runts, and comedian Jon Stewart. At night she might be out listening to a new band or at home trolling skateboarding blogs. Or she might be dining with REM singer Michael Stipe. In the past year, Bono has given shout-outs to McGrath at sold-out U2 concerts, thanking her for MTV's

Staying on top of pop culture trends requires relentless energy and a passion for hands-on research. McGrath, spends her off hours listening to new bands, reading new skateboarding blogs, or schmoozing with comedian Jon Stewart.

support of his AIDS and antipoverty campaign. And in a funny twist, she and *Rolling Stone* founder and publisher Jann S. Wenner, whose writers she idolized, are good pals.

BECOMING A "SUIT"

It's a long way from Scranton. Today the girl with a bohemian streak and rock 'n' roll dreams has one of the biggest and most challenging jobs in media. For much of her time at MTV, McGrath has been a nurturing manager of talent, a pop culture maven with a keen eye for what sells to kids—

> A trusted advisor with complementary skills, who can also act as a sounding board, can be a great asset. McGrath's right arm, a former media consultant, is academic cerebral, and has the know-how and connections to make the deals that MTV wants.

a "16-year-old boy trapped in an adult woman's body." Now she'll be less a "creative" and more of a "suit" (albeit accessorized with black Chuck Taylor sneakers and Urban Outfitters T-shirts). That's because Viacom split in two at the beginning of the year, pushing MTV and McGrath fully into the public eye. CBS went off as a separate company, leaving the new Viacom Inc., composed of Black Entertainment Television, the Paramount Pictures Corp. studios, and MTV Networks, which accounts for 85 percent of all the operating profits. What was a longtime partnership between McGrath and number one executive Tom Freston became a solo act, Freston [later fired] having ascended to the CEO job for all of Viacom. Freston, 60, jokes that his relationship with McGrath is the most enduring he's ever had with a woman. After all, they created MTV with folks like Robert W. Pittman, who went on to his rocky stint as a honcho at AOL Time Warner. Their wildly successful convergence play of 25 years ago put music and video improbably together and changed cable TV and music forever.

BREAK THROUGH THE CLUTTER

When the McGraths dropped their daughter off in New York in 1978 with no job prospects, they assured Judy, then 26 and armed with an English literature degree, that she would land on her feet. Soon she was writing stories for *Mademoiselle* with titles like "Models' Party Tips" and "Men Who Love Women Who Hate Men and Why." Like so many young people who come to New York teeming with ambition, McGrath found that life in the big city was the "ultimate high," she recalls, no matter how lean she was living—in this case, crammed into a Gramercy Park apartment with seven other women. Three years later, she was doing the "Dos and Don'ts" advice column for *Glamour* when friends, impressed with her turns of phrase, recommended her to Pittman. He hired McGrath to write promos that would give MTV a distinctive voice right out of the gate. Today McGrath is taking on her new role at a time when the very notions of hip and cutting-edge are being reinvented once again. You might say that her challenge is much as it was at her first job: to make MTV unique amid the media clutter.

The music channel may have seemed bold and experimental when it began in August 1981. But the MTV empire today is a staple of the media establishment and faces a slew of new threats. After all, this is the iPod era, a broadband world, and the online generation is defining for itself what is edgy and new. Ratings may be strong for many of the channels, but the original MTV isn't the must-see it once was. "We watch it because it's there," says Marie McGrory, a Manhattan tenth grader. Can McGrath keep her empire cool enough and nimble enough for Marie's generation and beyond?

Think about the cold dread the MTV chief and her coterie of aging hipster executives felt last summer when they heard that Rupert Murdoch had outbid MTV parent Viacom for Myspace.com. The exploding social networking community of 54 million registered young people would have been a perfect fit with MTV. Instead, for $580 million, it went to Murdoch, a steely competitor but hardly an arbiter of hip. The Murdoch deal was no mere acquisition; it was a red flag. In a rare stern message to her senior staff, according to one executive present, McGrath warned that MTV could no longer afford to miss opportunities like Myspace. Not when the old business models were blowing up and every week brought a new outlet for doing what MTV had done so well for years— capturing the niche.

Although MTV Networks has always relied on homegrown talent, it recognizes that it needs to move quickly if it wants to stay ahead in the digital age. So McGrath is snatching up or partnering with new Web properties.

"A DIGITAL MARSHALL PLAN"

So McGrath has declared "a digital Marshall Plan." It signals the end of the one-screen company. The troops must now deliver services across new broadband channels, over cell phones, and via video games. Because MTV is so tapped into its consumers—"we're more inside the heads of our audience than anybody else"—advertisers will stay with MTV, she insists. McGrath is willing to shake things up, too. At a company known for nurturing homegrown talent, she broke the mold last November and tapped media consultant Michael J. Wolf to be president and chief operating officer. She added the post of chief digital officer the same month. Nostalgia for the era when *Video Killed the Radio Star* (MTV's first music video), she says, is a distraction. "Nobody wants to be who they used to be, including us. Media identities, like market share, are up for grabs," McGrath told a gathering of her advertising and affiliate sales executives in Miami in early January 2006. "If we were launching today, the first song I'd tee up would be the [1980s band] Plimsouls' *Everywhere at Once.*"

THE RIGHT PARTNERS

No piece of the network is under as much fire as the core MTV channel. Its younger audiences are the most easily lured away in this age of do-it-yourself music mixes, podcasting, and streaming video. MTV's ratings growth was just 5 percent over the past three years, according to research outfit Bernstein & Co., while VH1, with an older, more loyal audience, grew 17 percent. Comedy Central pulled in a 10 percent gain, largely because of Stewart. Meanwhile, Nickelodeon's $1 billion in annual operating profits is fueled by sales of things like SpongeBob trinkets and Dora the Explorer dolls. "MTV turns 25 this year," says Peter Golder, an associate professor of marketing at New York University's Stern School of Business. "It's difficult to be a mature brand."

So McGrath is doing something alien to MTV's start-from-scratch culture: seeking acquisitions and partnerships. Last year, MTV Networks bought companies like the amateur short-film Web site IFILM Corp. and children's Web site Neopets, treasure troves with tens of millions of sticky users. IFILM just launched a show on VH1, and the Nickelodeon team is helping to design consumer products for Neopets. In January, McGrath announced a deal in which MTV is teaming with Microsoft Corp. to launch a music download service, URGE, later this year. Other forms of media are getting infusions, too, including the movie units at MTV (*Hustle & Flow*, *Murderball*) and Nickelodeon (Julia Roberts in *Charlotte's Web*, due to be in theaters for Christmas 2006). And never mind the culture wars: McGrath continues to break new ground with channels such as gay-and-lesbian-themed Logo, which so far is seen in 22 million homes, despite pushback from some distributors.

For McGrath, the networking never ceases. Her schedule for the week of the Grammy Awards in Los Angeles goes like this: a meeting with IFILM CEO Blair Harrison to discuss new projects (she decided to pass up the gala and gave him her tickets—the better to smooth the new relationship); a sit-down with Jeffrey Katzenberg of DreamWorks Animation SKG Inc., whose live-action movie business was sold to MTV's sister company Paramount; a tour of the studio's operations and discussions about a possible rollout of consumer products with DreamWorks; lunch with Jared Hess, director of the 2004 indie smash *Napoleon Dynamite*, to see if he might do some short-form work for MTV. Then a quick flight to Vail by week's end to meet with cable distributors during a ski outing.

THE SPACE TO BE CREATIVE

As she readies MTV for its changing game, McGrath finds herself a member of the small but growing club of women at the top of big media companies, joining Oprah, Martha, Walt Disney Co.'s Anne Sweeney, and a handful of others. Cable TV was supposed to be more open to new leadership, yet the path to the executive suite is still plenty steep. McGrath remembers being thrilled to attend her first industry lunch at New York's 21 Club in the early 1980s. But when she entered, she recalls, "some guy handed me his coat to check." As it turns out, McGrath gets much of the credit for fostering MTV's inclusive culture, all the better for risk taking and creativity. "There is less testosterone. It's not the system of the old Hollywood moguls where they are throwing chairs at each other," says Pittman. "It's about listening and accepting ideas wherever and whomever they come from."

Among the diverse staff of fashion-forward twentysomethings— think of those colors-of-the-world Benetton ads—rushing urgently in packs through the halls of MTV, McGrath just blends in. She wears designer suits, true, but she can hold her own with a roomful of hip-hoppers. She tries to go home most nights at a relatively sane hour to her daughter, Anna, 11, and her husband and stay-at-home dad, Michael Corbett, but she always lugs a bagful of scripts and tapes. After Anna's asleep, she peppers executives with Black Berry messages until well past midnight.

At the receiving end of those messages is often her new deputy, Wolf. The new president, 44, is everything she isn't: left-brained, slightly academic, a bit stiff in new jeans donned for his job as grown-up at the MTV party. Over a 20-year career at Booz Allen Hamilton Inc. and McKinsey & Co., Wolf has looked under the hood of nearly every major media outfit, although he never had a hands-on role. Wolf has a reputation as a brilliant strategist with an invaluable Rolodex, having helped dozens of CEOs navigate through the shoals of new media. He and McGrath met nearly 10 years ago, when MTV became a client.

Wolf's biggest assignment is to capture new digital dollars. Current online revenue is about $150 million, projected to grow to $500 million in three years. "Listen, the world has come to us, " says Wolf. "The Internet is no longer about text. It's about video. We produce and own more video than anybody." On any given day, he and his boss fuel up at Starbucks, sit on the big sofas in McGrath's office, and plot how to reengineer MTV. They might analyze the 30 to 40 potential deals on his desk. Or he'll recount his talks with advertisers. Right now, Wolf is crafting a plan with Honda Motor Co. to market cars to younger buyers across all MTV platforms. (Advertising brings in 60 percent of MTV revenues; distribution fees, 30 percent; consumer products, 10 percent.) "Advertisers would rather connect with that one alpha consumer [young trendsetter] vs. three beta consumers," he says. "We understand that audience, and we can help them do that."

Being an established brand can be a liability in the notoriously fickle youth market. McGrath keeps the company on the cutting edge by not playing it safe and championing content that will get buzz, whether it's *The Real World*, or Logo.

FIND THE NEW NIKES

His team is wielding the network's consumer research to win deals, for example, with the makers of must-have gadgets. Studies done for

While some companies see focus groups as the enemy of creativity, MTV Networks uses them as a tool. Research into preteens' cell phone usage by one of MTV's properties, for instance, helped the media company land a deal with AT&T to create a phone service for kids.

Nickelodeon recently found that kids aged 8 to 14 send an average of 14.4 text messages and make 8.8 calls on their cell phones a day. Executives at SBC Communications Inc., now AT&T Inc., were fascinated by these findings and have begun working with the kids' channel to develop a phone and services for preteens, says McGrath. Jason Hirschhorn, MTV's chief digital officer, is talking to everyone from Verizon Communications Inc. to Best Buy Co. about using MTV shows and characters. "Consumer electronics are the new Nikes," says Hirschhorn, 34. "Kids want their phones or their MP3 players to say something about who they are." So MTV helped Virgin Mobile Holdings and handset maker Kyocera Corp. design a new slider phone.

"ANYTHING IS POSSIBLE" SPIRIT

Reviewing the arc of any career, there's always a sense of inevitability. But serendipity played a big part in Judy McGrath's path to MTV. In 1980, Bob Pittman was an executive at Warner Amex Satellite Entertainment, a company that owned The Movie Channel and a few other media properties. His mission was to put music on cable TV. Pittman's then-wife, Sandy, worked at *Mademoiselle* and suggested a few colleagues whom her husband might want to hire. First he recruited Ann Foley, McGrath's friend and today an executive vice president of programming at Showtime Networks Inc. (part of the CBS side in the Viacom split). Then he hired Brown Johnson, who runs the Nick Jr. brand today under McGrath. A year later, Johnson and Foley sent him Judy.

As much as MTV shaped her, McGrath brought to her job a strong sense of community. If she has been "smart or lucky at one thing," McGrath says, "it has been [picking] good people." She attributes much of that to her parents' "everyman sensibility." Ann and Charles McGrath died on the same day four years apart in the 1980s. "They never really got to see or enjoy the ride," says McGrath. "But they are the reason I had an excellent start to life and why I made this great leap. I never knew anyone in the entertainment world and never could imagine I would be part of it like this." She's hard put to explain why she made it to the top of MTV instead of others, but she suggests that maybe it was about perseverance. "It's a really undervalued asset. It's not sexy, but if you really want something, you've got to hang in there," she says. "I never phoned it in. I have given my share of dogs' lives to this company."

Some of McGrath's biggest successes have come when she followed her gut. Although there was a lot of internal debate, McGrath launched MTV's Rock the Vote Campaign and invited the presidential candidates onto the network.

And if MTV is to stay a trendsetter, she'll have to maintain the same kind of anything-is-possible spirit she has encouraged since MTV's inception. The key, she says, is creating a space where people feel safe and aren't afraid to fail: "Falling flat on your face is a great motivator. So is accident." Her mantra: "The smartest thing we can do when confronted by something truly creative is to get out of the way." That's pretty much what happened when two young producers came to McGrath in the early 1990s with a new idea for a dramatic series that didn't require hiring actors or writers. McGrath was intrigued. The idea was to film seven people living in a New York City loft over several months, following the soap opera of their daily lives and dropping a soundtrack of new tunes behind it. MTV's *The Real World* debuted in 1992, and reality TV was born. Its seventeenth season is shooting now in Key West.

TRUST YOUR GUT

The scrappy Scranton girl also trusts her gut. There was much debate internally in the early 1990s about whether it was wise for MTV to entangle itself in politics. McGrath wanted to hold forums for the presidential candidates in 1992 and get kids engaged through the Rock the Vote campaign. She and others felt strongly that politicians needed to hear from kids. To keep up the momentum after Bill Clinton won, they decided to host an official inaugural ball. Certain that Clinton would never show, McGrath says that she was taken aback when she got word "about halfway through the show that Elvis is in the building," she recalls. "Clinton walks in, gets

As one of the few women to climb to the top of a media company, McGrath has fostered an open culture that promotes diversity. She hates it when people pander to her, and she welcomes ideas from everyone, whether interns or vice presidents.

onstage, and says, 'MTV had everything to do with my election.' It was the best."

Another flier she took was giving Jon Stewart a second chance in 1998 after MTV canceled an earlier show. When Craig Kilborn left *The Daily Show*, McGrath voted for Stewart as anchor. "There's just something about Jon Stewart, right?" she says. "The guy has a voice." McGrath is tight with Stewart, who has become so popular he hosts the Oscars. They talk by phone frequently, mostly chitchat about their kids. And McGrath is one of those rare people who can get Stewart to be serious—well, almost. "We all understand this is a business, but the quality of the content is everything with her," Stewart says of McGrath. Then he quickly shifts to full deadpan. He says he loves the freedom she has given him to extend the Jon Stewart brand. His latest idea: launching a line of casual wear. "It will be one outfit a week. You put it on on Monday mornings and take it off on Sunday nights." When told of Stewart's idea, McGrath guffaws: "Brilliant!"

INTUITIVE APPRECIATIONS

McGrath's hunger for fiction, movies, and music takes in both the highbrow and the lowbrow. One recent morning, she got up before the rest of the family in their brownstone on Manhattan's Upper West Side to read Kate Moses's *Wintering: A Novel of Sylvia Plath*. Several nights before, she stayed up for Madonna's 1991 concert tour documentary *Truth or Dare*, although her husband, Mike, begged her to turn the TV off and go to sleep. Whether it's rereading Samuel Beckett's novel *Malone Dies* or scarfing up the latest issue of *US Weekly*, friends say she is voracious. "[Judy] was the only person I ever worked with who knew as much about great literature as what was going on between East Coast and West Coast rappers," says former MTV executive Sara Levinson. "I always thought her intuitive appreciation of storytelling and characters was an enormous secret weapon."

It's the second day of the MTV retreat in Miami, and there's a new urgency in the CEO's message. McGrath praises her team for double-digit ad revenue growth in 2005. But she also warns against complacency in the face of game-changing innovation. In speeches and side conversations in hotel elevators, McGrath presses for MTV to shed its skin yet again and reimagine itself. She did that herself when she left Scranton and created a new life among New York's glitterati. This is the year that her old friend Freston will sell the new Viacom's prospects to Wall Street. So far investors are in a wait-and-see mood: the shares have been flat, at about $42, since the new Viacom began trading on its own on January 3.

PUSH THE ENVELOPE

McGrath knows that great, envelope-pushing programming is still the answer. That's why she carved out time one afternoon to do what she has done thousands of times, the thing she really loves: listen to a pitch. Three top Comedy Central executives met in a hotel suite with McGrath to review the slate of possible new shows for the year. The channel was sucker-punched last year when one of its biggest stars, Dave Chappelle, vanished in midseason. So Doug Herzog, who heads Comedy Central, Spike TV, and TV Land and is a close personal friend (he was a witness at her City Hall wedding), is hoping for a big hit to fill the void. (It turns out that the four shows that Chappelle taped before he bolted were ready later in the year, so Herzog slated them to be shown on Comedy Central's new broadband channel, Motherload.)

McGrath has the ability to recognize great talent (she hired Jon Stewart for the Comedy Channel, even after his previous show failed). Equally important, she doesn't micromanage or muzzle, giving people the freedom to be creative.

Michelle Ganeless, Comedy Central's general manager, shows McGrath a prospective scheduling grid for the year, explaining that advertising is looking exceptionally good for late spring. Lauren Corrao, Comedy Central's executive vice president of original programming, slips a DVD into a player to show McGrath the new stuff. Herzog, Ganeless, and Corrao are all MTV veterans, so the session is less a nerve-racking pitch than it is four friends eating chicken sandwiches and watching some new material together. First is a clip from *American Lives*, a part-scripted, part-improvised show about a TV news team in Spokane, Washington. NBC passed on it in 2005; Comedy Central scooped it up. Among the other shows:

a vehicle for politically incorrect comedian Sarah Silverman and Lewis Black's *Red State Diaries*. If that flies, it would be the third spin-off from *The Daily Show*, after Steven Colbert's *The Colbert Report*.

McGrath watches, laughs, listens to her team, laughs some more, but never takes notes. When it's over, she says, "Hey, guys, this looks really good," peering down again at the scheduling grid for the year ahead, one that she knows could be her most challenging yet. Then she tosses the paper aside and asks the really important question: do you think Jon Stewart can get us tickets to the Oscars?

MONDAY MORNING...

THE PROBLEM

Creating breakthrough products and content that appeal to a demographic whose tastes are constantly changing

Finding ways to adopt new platforms and dominate new markets in which the company has no expertise or experience

THE STRATEGY

Acquire businesses and form joint ventures with others that have the know-how that the organization needs if it is to succeed in emerging markets.

Use the organization's internal consumer research to inspire new programming, deals, and products.

Voraciously consume pop culture in order to stay on top of trends.

SUSTAINING THE WIN

Constantly encourage employees to reimagine and reinvent the brand to ensure that the company does not lapse into complacency.

INGVAR KAMPRAD: HOW IKEA BECAME A GLOBAL CULT BRAND

Courtesy of Getty Images.

POWER PLAYER

Not long after Ingvar Kamprad founded IKEA, he spelled out the company's mission: to create "a better life for many." Some 66 years later, IKEA has become one of the world's most successful mass-market retailers by selling high style at a low price.

This November 2005 cover story was reported by Kerry Capell, with Ariane Sains, Cristina Lindblad, Ann Therese Palmer, Jason Bush, Dexter Roberts, and Kenji Hall.

Seduce the shopper. Stores are set up to promote fun and ease of shopping.

Forge a bond with customers and give the company a strong brand identity through creative promotions.

Create the story. Build buzz to create evangelists for the brand around the world.

Create a megastore that serves as "curator," providing one-stop shopping for the design- and cost-conscious consumer.

Inspire the staff. Employees may not get rich, but they do enjoy autonomy, which inspires them to embrace the brand ethics of frugality and style that drive the company.

SEDUCE THE SHOPPER

When Roger Penguino heard that IKEA was offering $4,000 in gift certificates to the first person in line at the opening of its new Atlanta store, he had no choice. He threw a tent into the back of his car and sped down to the site. There, the 24-year-old Mac specialist with Apple Computer Inc. pitched camp, hunkered down, and waited. And waited. Seven broiling days later, when the store opened on June 29, more than 2,000 IKEA fanatics had joined him. Some were lured by the promise of lesser prizes for the first 100. Others were just there for the carnival atmosphere (somebody even brought a grill). The newly wed Penguino got his certificates and bagged a $799 Karlanda sofa and a $179 Malm bed, among other items. He also achieved celebrity status: "Whenever I go back, employees recognize me and show me the new stuff."

Penguino is a citizen of IKEA World, a state of mind that revolves around contemporary design, low prices, wacky promotions, and an enthusiasm that few institutions in or out of business can muster. Perhaps more than any other company in the world, IKEA has become a curator of people's lifestyles, if not their lives. At a time when consumers face so many choices for everything they buy, IKEA provides a one-stop sanctuary for coolness. It is a trusted safe zone that people can enter and immediately be part of a like-minded cost/design/environmentally sensitive global tribe. There are other would-be curators around—Starbucks and Virgin do a good job— but IKEA does it best.

If the Swedish retailer has its way, you too will live in a BoKlok home and sleep in a Leksvik bed under a Brunskära quilt. (Beds are named for Norwegian cities; bedding after flowers and plants. One disaster: a child's bed called Gutvik, which sounds like "good f***" in German.) IKEA wants to supply the food in your fridge (it also sells the fridge) and the soap in your shower.

Attracting customers and creating buzz for new stores is a major challenge for most retailers, but IKEA's store openings routinely attract huge crowds. The key: the company's creative, sometimes over-the-top publicity stunts.

FORGE A BOND WITH CUSTOMERS

The IKEA concept has plenty of room to run: the retailer accounts for just 5 to 10 percent of the furniture market in each country in which it operates. More important, says

CEO Anders Dahlvig, is that "awareness of our brand is much bigger than the size of our company." That's because IKEA is far more than a furniture merchant. It sells a lifestyle that customers around the world embrace as a signal that they've arrived, that they have good taste and recognize value. "If it wasn't for IKEA," writes British design magazine *Icon*, "most people would have no access to affordable contemporary design." The magazine even voted IKEA founder Ingvar Kamprad the most influential tastemaker in the world today.

As long as consumers from Moscow to Beijing and beyond keep striving to enter the middle class, there will be a need for IKEA. Think about it: what mass-market retailer has had more success globally? Not Wal-Mart Stores Inc., which despite its vast strengths has stumbled in Brazil, Germany, and Japan. Not France's Carrefour, which has never made it in the United States. IKEA has had its slip-ups, too. But right now its 226 stores in Europe, Asia, Australia, and the United States are thriving, hosting 410 million shoppers a year. The emotional response is unparalleled. The promise of store vouchers for the first 50 shoppers drew thousands to an IKEA store in the Saudi Arabian city of Jeddah in September 2004. In the ensuing melee, 2 people died and 16 were injured. A February opening in London attracted up to 6,000 before police were called in.

> In a world in which consumers face a bewildering array of choices, IKEA stands out. By offering comfortably wide aisles, a playroom for kids, and a restaurant in every store, it makes the shopping experience a pleasurable outing, not drudgery.

CREATE THE STORY

Why the uproar? IKEA is the quintessential global cult brand. Just take those stunts. Before the Atlanta opening, IKEA managers invited locals to apply for the post of Ambassador of Kul (Swedish for fun). The five winners wrote an essay on why they deserved $2,000 in vouchers. There was one catch: they would have to live in the store for three days before the opening, take part in contests, and sleep in the bedding department. "I got about eight hours of sleep total because of all the drilling and banging going on," says winner Jordan Leopold, a manager at Costco Wholesale.

Leopold got his bedroom set. And IKEA got to craft another story about itself—a story picked up in the press that drew even more

What distinguishes Kamprad is his ability to formulate a clear vision for IKEA and integrate it thoroughly into the corporate culture. Whether through IKEA's "Antibureaucracy Weeks," or his insistence on flying economy class, Kamprad has led by example.

shoppers. More shoppers, more traffic. More traffic, more sales. More sales, more buzz. A new store in Bolingbrook, Illinois, near Chicago, is expected to generate some $2.5 million in tax revenues, so the town is paying down debt and doing away with some local levies.

Such buzz has kept IKEA's sales growing at a healthy clip: For the fiscal year 2005, revenues rose 15 percent, to $17.7 billion. And although privately held IKEA guards its profit figures as jealously as its recipe for Swedish meatballs, analyst Mattias Karlkjell of Stockholm's ABG Sundal Collier conservatively estimates IKEA's pretax operating profits at $1.7 billion. IKEA maintains these profits even while it cuts prices steadily. "IKEA's operating margins of approximately 10 percent are among the best in home furnishings," Karlkjell says. They also compare well with margins of 5 percent at Pier 1 Imports and 7.7 percent at Target, both competitors of IKEA in the United States.

KEEP THE BUZZ

To keep growing at that pace, IKEA is accelerating its store rollouts. Nineteen new outlets are set to open worldwide in the fiscal year ending August 31, 2006, at a cost of $66 million per store, on average. CEO Dahlvig is keen to boost IKEA's profile in three of its fastest-growing markets: the United States, Russia (IKEA is already a huge hit in Moscow), and China (now worth $120 million in sales). In the United States, he figures the field is wide open: "We have 25 stores in a market the size of Europe, where we have more than 160 stores." The goal is 50 U.S. outlets by 2010. Five have opened in 2005, up from just one in 2000.

The key to these rollouts is to preserve the strong enthusiasm that IKEA evokes, an enthusiasm that has inspired two case studies from Harvard Business School and endless shopper comments on the Net. Examples: "IKEA makes me free to become what I want to be" (from Romania). Or this: "Half my house is from IKEA—and the nearest store is six hours away" (the United States). Or this: "Every time, it's trendy for less money" (Germany).

CREATE A MEGASTORE

What enthralls shoppers and scholars alike is the store visit—a similar experience the world over. The blue-and-yellow buildings average 300,000 square feet in size, about equal to five football fields. The sheer number of items—7,000, from kitchen cabinets to candlesticks—is a decisive advantage. "Others offer affordable furniture," says Bryan Roberts, research manager at Planet Retail, a consultancy in London. "But there's no one else who offers the whole concept in the big shed."

While globalization may be bringing the world's cultures closer, there are still huge national and ethnic differences that affect what people want to buy. IKEA meets the market challenge by listening closely to its customers—all of them. IKEA researches how people actually live and designs products that suit consumers.

The global middle class that IKEA targets shares buying habits. The $120 Billy bookcase, $13 Lack side table, and $190 Ivar storage system are best-sellers worldwide. (U.S. prices are used throughout this chapter.) Spending per customer is even similar. According to IKEA, the figure in Russia is $85 per store visit—exactly the same as in affluent Sweden.

Wherever they are, customers tend to think of the store visit as more of an outing than a chore. That's intentional; as one of the Harvard B-school studies states, IKEA practices a form of "gentle coercion" to keep you as long as possible. Right at the entrance, for example, you can drop off your kids at the playroom, an amenity that encourages more leisurely shopping.

Then, clutching your dog-eared catalog (the print run for the 2006 edition was 160 million—more than the Bible, IKEA claims), you proceed along a marked path through the warren of showrooms. "Because the store is designed as a circle, I can see everything as long as I keep walking in one direction," says Krystyna Gavora, an architect who frequents the IKEA store in Schaumburg, Illinois. Wide aisles let you inspect the merchandise without holding up traffic. The furniture itself is arranged in fully accessorized displays, right down to the picture frames on the nightstand, to inspire customers and get them to spend more. The settings are so lifelike that one writer is staging a play at IKEA in Renton, Washington.

Along the way, one touch after another seduces the shopper, from the paper measuring tapes and pencils to strategically placed bins with items like pink plastic watering cans, scented candles, and picture frames. These are things you never knew you needed, but at less than $2 each, you load up on them anyway. You set out to buy a $40 coffee table, but you end up dropping $500 on everything from storage units to glassware. "They have this way of making you believe nothing is expensive," says Bertille Faroult, a shopper at IKEA on the outskirts of Paris. The bins and shelves constantly hold surprises: IKEA replaces a third of its product line every year.

Then there's the stop at the restaurant, which is usually placed at the center of the store to give shoppers a breather and encourage them to keep going. You proceed to the warehouse, where the full genius of founder Kamprad is on display. Nearly all the big items are flat-packed, which not only saves IKEA millions in shipping costs from suppliers but also enables shoppers to haul their own stuff home—another savings. Finally, you have the fun (or agony) of assembling your purchases at home, equipped with nothing but an Allen wrench and those cryptic instructions.

Finding ways to cut costs without diminishing quality is an age-old concern for retailers, but it has become more critical because of increased competition and more bargain-hungry shoppers. IKEA sells products at ever-lower prices by encouraging unconventional thinking and problem solving.

A vocal minority rails at IKEA for its long lines, crowded parking lots, exasperating assembly experiences, and furniture that's hardly built for the ages (the running joke is that IKEA is Swedish for particleboard). But the converts outnumber the critics. And for every fan who shops at IKEA, there seems to be one working at the store itself. The fanaticism stems from founder Kamprad, 79, a figure as important to global retailing as Wal-Mart's Sam Walton. Kamprad started the company in 1943 at the age of 17, selling pens, Christmas cards, and seeds from a shed on his family's farm in southern Sweden.

In 1951, the first catalog appeared (Kamprad wrote all the text himself until 1963). His credo of creating "a better life for many" is enshrined in his almost evangelical 1976 tract, *A Furniture Dealer's Testament*. Peppered with folksy tidbits—"divide your life into 10-minute units and sacrifice as few as possible in meaningless activity," "wasting resources is a mortal sin" (that's for sure: employees are the catalog models), or the more revealing "it is our duty to expand"—the pamphlet is given to all employees the day they start.

INSPIRE THE STAFF

Kamprad, though officially retired, is still the cheerleader for the practices that define IKEA culture. One is egalitarianism. IKEA regularly stages Antibureaucracy Weeks, during which executives work on the shop floor or tend the registers. "In February," says CEO Dahlvig, "I was unloading trucks and selling beds and mattresses."

KEEP PRICES LOW

Another feature is a steely competitiveness. You get a sense of that at one of IKEA's main offices, in Helsingborg, Sweden. At the doorway, a massive bulletin board tracks weekly sales growth, names the best-performing country markets, and identifies the best-selling furniture. The other

> Customer focus is so intense that even senior managers must work behind the registers and in the warehouse for stints each year.

message that comes across loud and clear: cut prices. At the far end of the Helsingborg foyer is a row of best-selling Klippan sofas, displaying models from 1999 to 2006 with their euro price tags. In 1999 the Klippan was $354. In 2006 it will be $202.

The montage vividly illustrates IKEA's relentless cost cutting. The retailer aims to lower prices across its entire offering by an average of 2 to 3 percent each year. It goes deeper when it wants to hit rivals in certain segments. "We look at the competition, take their price, and then slash it in half," says Mark McCaslin, manager of IKEA Long Island, in Hicksville, New York.

It helps that frugality is as deeply ingrained in the corporate DNA as the obsession with design. Managers fly economy, even top brass. Steen Kanter, who left IKEA in 1994 and now heads his own retail consultancy in Philadelphia, Kanter International, recalls that while flying with Kamprad once, the boss handed him a coupon for a car rental he had ripped out of an in-flight magazine.

This cost obsession is fused with the design culture. "Designing beautiful-but-expensive products is easy," says Josephine Rydberg-Dumont, president of IKEA of Sweden. "Designing beautiful products that are inexpensive and functional is a huge challenge."

No design—no matter how inspired—finds its way into the showroom if it cannot be made affordable. To achieve that goal, the company's 12 full-time designers at Almhult, Sweden, along with 80 freelancers, work hand in hand with in-house production teams to identify the appropriate materials and least costly suppliers, a trial-and-error process that can take as long as three years. Example: for the PS Ellan, a $39.99 dining room chair that can rock back on its hind legs without tipping over, designer Chris Martin worked with production staff for a year and a half to adapt a wood-fiber composite, an inexpensive blend of wood chips and plastic resin used in highway noise barriers, for use in furnishings. Martin also had to design the chair to break down into six pieces, so that it could be flat-packed and snapped together without screws.

With a network of 1,300 suppliers in 53 countries, IKEA works overtime to find the right manufacturer for each product. It once contracted with ski makers—experts in bent wood—to manufacture its Poang armchairs, and it has tapped makers of supermarket carts to turn out durable sofas. Simplicity, a tenet of Swedish design, helps keep costs down. For example, the 50-cent Trofé mug comes only in blue and white, the least expensive pigments. IKEA's conservation drive extends naturally from this cost cutting. For its new PS line, it challenged 28 designers to find innovative uses for discarded and unusual materials. The results: a table fashioned from reddish-brown birch heartwood (furniture makers prefer the pale exterior wood) and a storage system made from recycled milk cartons.

If sales keep growing at their historical average, by 2010 IKEA will need to source twice as much material as today. "We can't increase by more than 20 stores a year because supply is the bottleneck," says Lennart Dahlgren, country manager for Russia. Since Russia is a source of timber, IKEA aims to turn it into a major supplier of finished products.

Adding to the challenge, the suppliers and designers have to customize some IKEA products to make them sell better in local markets. In China, the 250,000 plastic placemats that IKEA produced to commemorate the year of the rooster sold out in just three weeks. Julie Desrosiers, the bedroom-line manager at IKEA of Sweden, visited people's houses in the United States and Europe to peek into their closets, learning that "Americans prefer to store most of their clothes folded, and Italians like to hang." The result was

Keep prices low by maintaining an ethic of frugality and seeking innovative ways to manufacture products.

a wardrobe that features deeper drawers for U.S. customers.

The American market poses special challenges for IKEA because of the huge differences within the United States. "It's so easy to forget the reality of how people live," says IKEA's U.S. interior design director, Mats Nilsson. In the spring of 2004, IKEA realized that it might not be reaching California's Hispanics. So its designers visited the homes of Hispanic staff. They soon realized that they had set up the store's displays all wrong. Large Hispanic families need dining tables and sofas that fit more than two people, the Swedish norm. They prefer bold colors to the more subdued Scandinavian palette, and they display tons of pictures in elaborate frames. Nilsson warmed up the showrooms' colors, added more seating, and threw in numerous picture frames.

Instead of pointing fingers or trying to cover up mistakes, IKEA studies its failures closely and strives to learn from them. Analyzing why its U.S. expansion efforts in the early 1990s were disappointing, IKEA managers pinpointed weak spots and were able to correct them. While every company wants to avoid stumbles, the reality is that it is impossible to continue to grow without taking risks, making errors, and understanding what went wrong.

IKEA is particularly concerned about the United States, since it's key to the company's expansion—and since IKEA came close to blowing it. "We got our clocks cleaned in the early 1990s because we really didn't listen to the consumer," says Kanter. Its stores weren't big enough to offer the full IKEA experience, and many of them were in poor locations. Prices were too high. Beds were measured in centimeters, not king, queen, and twin. Sofas weren't deep enough, curtains were too short, and kitchens didn't fit U.S.-size appliances. "American customers were buying vases to drink from because the glasses were too small," recalls Goran Carstedt, the former head of IKEA North America, who helped engineer a turnaround. Parts of the product line were adapted (no more metric measurements), new and bigger store locations chosen, prices slashed, and service improved. Now U.S. managers are paying close attention to the tiniest details. "Americans want more comfortable sofas, higher-quality textiles, bigger glasses, more spacious entertainment units," says Pernille Spiers-Lopez, head of IKEA North America.

Can the cult keep thriving? IKEA has stumbled badly before. A foray into Japan 30 years ago was a disaster (the Japanese wanted high quality and great materials, not low price and particleboard). The company is just now gearing up for a return to Japan next year. IKEA is also seeing more competition than ever. In the United States, Target has recruited top designer Thomas O'Brien to develop a range of low-priced furnishings, which were launched in October. Kmart has been collaborating with Martha Stewart on its own furniture line. An IKEA-like chain called Fly is popular in France. In Japan, Nitori Co. has a lock on low-cost furniture.

Perhaps the bigger issue is what happens inside IKEA. "The great challenge of any organization as it becomes larger and more diverse is how to keep the core founding values alive," says Harvard Business School Professor Christopher A. Bartlett, author of a 1996 case study. IKEA is still run by managers who were trained and groomed by Kamprad himself—and who are personally devoted to the founder. As the direct links with Kamprad disappear, the culture may start to fade.

For now, the founder's legacy is alive and well. The Klippan couches are selling briskly. New lines of foods, travel gear, and toiletries are due soon. IKEA is gearing up for its Christmas tree promotion— you buy a live tree, then return it for a rebate (and end up shopping at IKEA in the slow month of January).

And the fans keep clamoring for more. At least once a year, Jen Segrest, a 36-year-old freelance Web designer, and her husband travel 10 hours round trip from their home in Middletown, Ohio, to IKEA in Schaumburg, Illinois, near Chicago. "Every piece of furniture in my living room is IKEA—except for an end table, which I hate. And next time I go to IKEA I'll replace it," says Segrest. To lure the retailer to Ohio, Segrest has even started a blog called OH! IKEA. The banner on the home page reads "IKEA in Ohio—Because man cannot live on Target alone."

MONDAY MORNING...

MONDAY

THE PROBLEM

Developing products that will appeal to taste-conscious and price-sensitive consumers around the world

Finding a way to keep drawing crowds to the stores, even while the number of large competitors continues to grow

THE SOLUTION

Encourage employees to dream up unorthodox ways to make stylish goods at low prices.

Explore and study regional and cultural differences among consumers and devise products that will fit the way they actually live.

Launch humorous, off-the-wall publicity stunts to lure customers to stores, and keep them happy while they're there by designing a store that makes shopping fun.

SUSTAINING THE WIN

Closely analyze your missteps and blunders so that you can make the necessary corrections and continue taking the risks you need to grow the company.

JEFF IMMELT:
DEMANDING MORE RISK AND
INNOVATION FROM GE

©Len Irish

POWER PLAYER

General Electric has been long admired for its steady focus on cost cutting, efficiency, and the bottom line. But Jeffrey R. Immelt, is overhauling the culture, changing everything from how often managers are reassigned to GE's portfolio. The goal: to make bold ideas and sophisticated marketing part of the company's DNA.

In this profile from March 2005, Diane Brady reports on Jeffrey Immelt's mission to transform GE.

Create a cultural revolution with a more global workforce.

Generate blockbuster ideas by funding "Imagination Breakthrough" projects, ventures proposed by managers that will extend the company's boundaries.

Inspire employees to focus on customer satisfaction and new ideas by linking bonuses to sales growth, with less emphasis on bottom-line results.

Rejigger GE's portfolio so as to acquire business in new hot areas.

Push the envelope to achieve immediate growth from existing businesses.

Hire outsiders with the necessary skills, experience, and mindset to serve as the new model for leadership.

CREATE A CULTURAL REVOLUTION

Despite his air of easy-going confidence, Jeffrey R. Immelt admits to two fears: that General Electric Co. will become boring and that his top people might act like cowards. That's right: cowards. He worries that GE's famous obsession with bottom-line results—and its tendency to get rid of those individuals who don't meet them— will make some executives shy away from taking risks that could revolutionize the company.

Immelt is clearly pushing for a cultural revolution. For several years the GE chairman and CEO has been on a mission to transform the hard-driving, process-oriented company into one that is steeped in creativity and wired for growth. He wants to move GE's average organic growth rate—the increase in revenue that comes from existing operations, rather than from deals and currency fluctuations—to at least 8 percent from about 5 percent over the past decade. Under his former boss, the renowned Jack Welch, the skills that GE prized above all others were cost cutting, efficiency, and deal making. What mattered was the continual improvement of operations, and that mindset helped make the $152 billion industrial and financial behemoth a marvel of earnings consistency. Immelt hasn't turned his back on the old ways. But in his GE, the new imperatives are risk taking, sophisticated marketing, and, above all, innovation.

This change is born of necessity. The Welch era reached its zenith in the booming, anything-goes economy of the late 1990s. Back then, GE always seemed to beat the consensus forecasts by a penny a share—and investors felt no burning need to figure out exactly how the company did it. Immelt has no such luxury. With a slower-growing domestic economy, less tolerance among investors for buying the way to growth, and more global competitors, Immelt, like many of his peers, has been forced to shift the emphasis from deals and cost cutting to new products, services, and markets. Any other course risks a slow descent into irrelevance. "It's a different era," says Immelt, a natural salesman who still happily recounts the days when he drove around his territory in a Ford Taurus while at GE Plastics. He knows that the world looks to GE as a harbinger of future trends, says Ogilvy & Mather Worldwide Chief Executive Rochelle B. Lazarus, who sits on the GE board. "He really feels that GE has a responsibility to get out in front and play a leadership role."

HIRING OUTSIDERS

So how, exactly, do you make a culture as ingrained as GE's sizzle with bold thinking and creative energy? To start with, you banish some long-cherished traditions and beliefs. Immelt has welcomed outsiders into the highest ranks, even making one of them, Sir William M. Castell, a vice chairman. That's a serious break with GE's promote-from-within past. He is pushing hard for a more global workforce that reflects the communities in which GE operates. Immelt is also encouraging his homegrown managers to become experts in their industries rather than just experts in managing. Instead of relying on executives who barely had time to position a family photo on their desk before moving on to their next assignment, he's diversifying the top ranks and urging his lieutenants to stay put and make a difference where they are.

GENERATING BLOCKBUSTER IDEAS

Most of all, Immelt has made the need to generate blockbuster ideas more than an abstract concept. In true GE fashion, he has engineered a quantifiable and scalable process for coming up with money-making "eureka!" moments. While Welch was best known for the annual Session C meetings, during which he personally evaluated the performance of GE's top several hundred managers, Immelt's highest-profile new gathering is the Commercial Council. Immelt leads this group of roughly a dozen top sales and marketing executives, along with some unit heads such as GE Consumer Finance CEO David R. Nissen. The members hold phone meetings every month and meet each quarter to discuss growth strategies, think up ways to reach customers, and evaluate ideas from the senior ranks that aim to take GE out on a limb. "Jeff has launched us on a journey to become one of the best sales and marketing companies in the world," says Nissen, who describes the meetings as collegial and more experimental than other GE gatherings.

This is no free-for-all, however. Business leaders must submit at least three "Imagination Breakthrough" proposals per

> To create the groundwork for the new GE, Immelt immediately focused on repositioning the company's portfolio. He committed to selling off the less profitable businesses, while buying into new industries with high growth potential.

Immelt is working to make the company more globally focused by creating and investing heavily in GE research centers in Bangalore, Shanghai, and Munich.

year that ultimately go before the council for review and discussion. The projects, which will receive billions in funding in the coming years, have to take GE into a new line of business, geographic area, or customer base. Oh, and each one has to give GE incremental growth of at least $100 million.

This kind of change can be scary stuff for folks steeped in Six Sigma, who were led to believe that if you made your numbers and were prepared to uproot your family every year or two, you had a shot at the top rungs. Now these people are being asked to develop real prowess in areas that are harder to measure, such as creativity, strategy, and customer service. They are being told to embrace risky ventures, many of which may fail. Immelt's GE can be seen as a grand experiment, still in its early days, to determine whether bold innovation can thrive in a productivity-driven company.

LINKING BONUSES TO SALES GROWTH

To inspire the fresh thinking he's looking for, Immelt is wielding the one thing that speaks loud and clear: money. The GE chief is tying executives' compensation to their ability to come up with ideas, improve customer service, generate cash growth, and boost sales instead of simply meeting bottom-line targets. As Immelt puts it, "You're not going to stick around this place and not take bets." More concretely, 20 percent of 2005 bonuses were to be based on meeting preestablished measures of how well a business is improving its ability to meet customer needs. And while he hasn't exactly repudiated Welch's insistence that managers cull the bottom 10 percent of their staff, insiders say that there's more flexibility and more subjectivity to the process. Risking failure is a badge of honor at GE these days.

A NEW PORTFOLIO

To lay the groundwork for an organization that grows through innovation, Immelt took steps early on to rejigger GE's portfolio. He committed to selling $15 billion of less profitable businesses, such as insurance, while shelling out more than $60 billion for acquisitions in hot areas, such as bioscience, cable and film entertainment, security, and wind power, that have better growth prospects. In doing so, he pared the low-margin, slower-growth businesses like appliances and lighting, which he diplomatically calls "cash generators" instead of "losers," down to 10 percent of the portfolio, from 33 percent in 2000. Nicole M. Parent of Credit Suisse First Boston is impressed with "the way they have been able to evolve the portfolio in such a short time" and with so little disruption. "This is a company where managers will do anything to achieve their goals."

> Building on existing businesses is far more cost-effective than making acquisitions. So Immelt isn't just talking about the need for new ideas. He is mandating that top managers propose at least three "Imagination Breakthrough" projects that will move the company into a new territory or line of business.

That's a good thing, because their back-slapping chief is now looking for "those things that grow the boundaries of this company." He's confident that the new business mix and growth incentives are already paying off. At GE's annual gathering of its top 650 executives in Boca Raton, Florida, in January 2005, he insisted that "there's never been a better day, a better time, or a better place to be [at GE]!" Strong words for a company that stretches back 127 years to founder Thomas Edison. After an 18 percent jump in revenues and earnings in the fourth quarter of 2005, to $43.7 billion and $5.4 billion, respectively, Immelt predicted up to 17 percent earnings growth and 10 percent sales gains for all of 2005, with double-digit returns in 2006. While economists were scratching their heads over the next quarter, Immelt was promising two years of explosive growth. No wonder Sharon Garavel, a quality leader at GE Commercial Finance, says that, at Boca, "everyone was talking about a $60 stock price," or about $24 more than the stock's price at that time.

That may be a stretch of the imagination for now, but Immelt is trying to recast the company for decades to come. He's spending big bucks to create the kind of infrastructure that can equip and foster an army of dreamers. That means beefing up GE's research facilities, creating something akin to a global brain trust that GE can tap to spur innovation. He has sunk $100 million into overhauling the

Determined to make great marketing and customer service integral to everyone's job, Immelt appointed a chief marketing officer, who instituted many programs, including sending GE's best marketers throughout the organization to evangelize and offered marketing courses.

company's research center in Niskayuna, New York, and forked out for cutting-edge centers in Bangalore, Shanghai, and Munich.

Globalizing research has allowed GE to get closer to its overseas customers. The simple fact is that most of GE's future growth will come from outside the United States. Immelt predicts that developing countries will account for 60 percent of the company's growth in the next 10 years, vs. about 20 percent during the past decade. But he is also spreading new practices to lethargic economies such as Germany. After a 2002 meeting with German Chancellor Gerhard Schröder reinforced his notion that GE could be doing more in that country, Immelt decided to open the Munich center. As Immelt explains, "There's no place in GE where you feel more like a loser than in Germany. You have Siemens and Philips, and we haven't been that good." By July 2004, a new center was up, and the results were immediate. According to Nani Beccalli-Falco, CEO of GE International, the company saw a 21.5 percent growth in German-speaking markets last year from 2003.

PUSHING THE ENVELOPE OF EXISTING BUSINESSES

Now that Immelt has repositioned the portfolio and added resources, his main objective is to get more immediate growth out of the businesses he already has. That's where the Imagination Breakthroughs come in. Immelt has agreed to invest $5 billion in 80 projects ranging from creating microjet engines to overhauling the brand image of 3,000 consumer-finance locations. The hope is that the first lot will generate $25 billion in revenue by 2007—cheap if it works, when you consider what it would cost to acquire something from the outside with that level of sales. In the next year or two, Immelt expects to have 200 such projects under way.

The pressure to produce could not be more intense. Many of the company's 307,000 workers weren't exactly hired to be part of a diverse, creative, fleet-footed army of visionaries who are acutely sensitive to customers' needs. "These guys just aren't dreamer types," says one consultant who has worked with the company. "It almost seems painful to them, like a waste of time." Even insiders who are openly euphoric about the changes under Chairman Jeff admit to feeling some fear in the depth of their guts.

"This is a big fundamental structural change, and that can be tough," says Paul T. Bossidy, CEO of GE Commercial Equipment Financing, who is reorganizing his sales force so that each person represents all of GE to particular customers. Susan P. Peters, GE's vice president for executive development, even talks about the need for employees to "reconceptualize" themselves. "What you have been to date isn't good enough for tomorrow," she says. Ouch.

To Immelt, the best managers are great marketers, not just great operators. That's a rethinking of GE's long-held bias that winning products essentially sell themselves. Beth Comstock, who was appointed chief marketing officer three years ago with the mission of boosting the company's marketing expertise, says that when she started, a number of insiders were skittish about the new agenda: "Everyone thought, 'I've got to get into sales and marketing to be relevant in this company.'"

Well, yes. Comstock is trying to elevate the role of marketing throughout GE. She has helped develop a commercial leadership program that sends the best and brightest marketers around the organization for two intensive years of training, much as GE's corporate audit staff has long done on the finance side. The auditors were important to maintaining financial discipline under Welch. Now, GE has initiated new courses in marketing, as well as courses on how to spark idea generation. Some executives have also taken to holding "idea jams," where people from diverse businesses brainstorm. Within GE Energy alone, there are "growth heroes" who are held up as emblematic of where the company wants to go, a "virtual idea box" to spur brainstorming via the Web, and "Excellerator awards" for the development of ideas. The jargon may smack of classic GE, but the approach is novel. "This is about unlocking the curiosity, yet having the rigor stay intact," says Comstock.

> One surefire way to motivate employees to change is to offer financial rewards. Immelt is linking managers' bonuses to their ability to develop new ideas, improve customer satisfaction, and increase sales growth.

In this era, marketing is not just a matter of producing edgier commercials or catchier slogans. It means getting outside the company to understand markets and customers. Among other things, GE's top marketing executives have spent a lot of time examining the practices of companies such as Procter & Gamble Co., which let them spend time last November in "The GYM," where strategies and issues are debated, examined, and maybe even solved. "The idea is to enhance a team's creative thinking," says P&G spokesman Terry Loftus. GE staffers also spent time at FedEx Corp., which has exceptional customer service. Welch did the same thing in benchmarking Motorola Inc. when he delved into Six Sigma, but the external focus is even stronger now.

Immelt wants his managers to lead industries rather than merely follow demand. Take the company's move to create a cleaner coal plant—another Imagination Breakthrough—before its customers were even asking for it. GE initiated the push after acquiring ChevronTexaco Corp.'s gasification-technology business last year. Immelt and GE Energy CEO John G. Rice brought together big power customers and experts on subjects such as climate change at GE's education center in Croton-on-Hudson, New York, in July 2004 to debate where the industry would be in 2015. James E. Rogers, chairman and CEO of public utilities giant Cinergy Corp., was shocked to hear Immelt talk about the need to generate electricity with far fewer emissions—a touchy subject in an industry that still burns a lot of coal. "He was unafraid to articulate a point of view that his customers might not share," says Rogers, whose company burns 30 million tons of coal a year.

Shaking up a culture as tradition-bound as that of GE often requires the help of outsiders, who will challenge the status quo and bring in new skills. Immelt hired more than 1,700 new sales and marketing employees.

What convinced Rogers to partner with GE and Bechtel Corp. on developing a cleaner coal power plant was the prospect of having an integrated package managed by GE. Instead of forcing Rogers to license the technology and figure it out himself, GE in partnership with Bechtel will design and implement the plan, while Cinergy will provide and help develop the site. GE's promise: that the cleaner-burning plant will soon become competitive with pulverized coal and that GE will handle any hiccups in the process. "I like the way they're thinking about the future," says Rogers. "They're going to make this work."

NEW HIRES, NEW IDEAS

But there's a limit to how much Immelt can transform his own people. A key strategy—and one that amounts to a gut punch to the culture— involves bringing in more outsiders. In sales and marketing alone, GE has hired more than 1,700 new faces in the past few years, including hundreds of seasoned veterans such as David J. Slump, a former ABB Group executive who is the chief marketing officer of GE Energy. "I just didn't think outsiders would do well here," says Slump, who was surprised at the unit's openness to changing its ways, though one of the senior executives did warn him about coming across as "too intense." That said, he was also amazed at the lack of attention to marketing when he arrived—there were no marketers among the senior ranks and no real sense of strategy beyond the occasional ad or product push. Slump felt needed.

Immelt is also looking for more leaders who are intensely passionate about their businesses and are experts in the details. "I want to see our people become part of their industries," he says. No one represents Immelt's vision of what a GE leader should be better than Bill Castell, who has spent his entire career in one industry and has rarely, if ever, focused on maximizing profits. The cerebral Brit was heading up diagnostics-and-bioscience giant Amersham PLC when Immelt acquired it (after much wooing) for $10.7 billion. Not only did Immelt make Castell head of the new $14 billion GE Healthcare, but he named him a vice chairman of GE and located the unit's headquarters outside the United States, in the English village of Chalfont St. Giles.

Castell is quite unlike the archetypal GE executive. He's totally immersed in his industry, a leading thinker on the future of personalized medicine who will never head up a business based on jet engines or commercial finance. Nor is he pursuing a black belt in Six Sigma or losing sleep over making his numbers. "People were surprised at first that I didn't tend to talk about the quarter," admits Castell. Yet Immelt loves him. "I want managers to have the kind of curiosity that Bill has, his passion for the industry," he says. "He understands where the market is going." This is, after all, a man who has been known to call up his boss and wax on about an angiogenesis marker that won't hit the marketplace for 10 years. Imagine how long that conversation would have lasted with Welch.

To encourage that kind of expertise and passion in the rest of his organization, Immelt is urging people to stay in one place longer to build stronger relationships with customers and markets. GE Energy's Rice—a hotshot who is emblematic of the old system, in which a great GE manager could parachute onto the scene to turn any business into gold—notes that the idea of staying put takes some adjustment. "There was always an impression in the midlevel ranks that if you weren't moving every few years, something was wrong," says Rice. He now says he likes the fact that he has been in one place for four years, because he's developing a deeper knowledge.

Investors are still waiting to see whether GE's evangelizing chairman can truly make his company grow faster than the world around it. Even some of his fans think that GE's new momentum has more to do with the overall economy than with idea generation. Says Steve Roukis of Matrix Asset Advisors, which owns 2 million GE shares: "If you have a revolutionary decade of growth around the world, who's going to be there to capture it? GE."

POWER MOVE

A major goal of Immelt's is to create a workforce that has a deep understanding of not only the company's markets but also its customers. As a result, he is doing away with the GE practice of rotating managers frequently and is encouraging them to stay put.

Capture it? Jeff Immelt wants to shape it, drive it, make it his own. For him, reinventing GE is the only way to make his company dominate this century, much as it led the one before.

MONDAY MORNING...

THE PROBLEM

Remaking the deeply ingrained values of a well-established company so that marketing is central to its mission

Stimulating groundbreaking ideas that will move the company into new geographic areas and markets

THE SOLUTION

Build up research centers in the United States and abroad that will serve as incubators for ideas and enable GE to get to know its overseas customers.

Emphasize the importance of marketing by appointing a chief marketing officer to spearhead various initiatives.

Create new programs in which managers are challenged to develop new business proposals, while also offering clear financial rewards for meeting new goals.

SUSTAINING THE WIN

Maintain the culture of innovation by applauding those who have the courage to risk failure in order to achieve big wins.

MARISSA MAYER:
MANAGING GOOGLE'S IDEA FACTORY

©Martin Klimek

POWER PLAYER

A headhunter persuaded Marissa Mayer to join Google, Inc. in 1999 as a programmer—Google's twentieth employee. Now, Marissa Mayer is charged with making sure that the tech giant continues to crank out brilliant ideas, even as clever competitors are hatching their own.

In this 2005 story, Ben Elgin looks at how Google outthinks its rivals.

Nurture great ideas from all levels of the company, not just the top.

Be available to employees so that they have an opportunity to get their ideas heard.

Demand creativity by giving employees "free thinking time" to develop pet projects, no matter how far from the company's central vision.

Acquire good ideas. Although preferring to develop new technologies in house, Google is also willing to snap up small companies with interesting initiatives.

CHAMPION OF INNOVATION

In late 1998, when Marissa Mayer first heard about a small outfit called Google, she hardly batted an eye. The Stanford University graduate student was encouraged by her advisor to check out the research of two guys on the computer science building's fourth floor who were developing ways to analyze the World Wide Web.

But Internet start-ups were as common as hay fever in Silicon Valley. Mayer, then 23, was leaning in another direction. She was considering taking a teaching gig at Carnegie Mellon University. And the thought of joining up with some of the university's techies wasn't exactly appealing. "I knew about the Stanford Ph.D. types," she muses. "They love to Rollerblade. They eat pizza for breakfast. They don't shower much. And they don't say 'Sorry' when they bump into you in the hallway."

Fortunately for both Google Inc. and Mayer, she had a change of heart. Since joining Google, Mayer has emerged as a powerful force inside the high-flying company. Her title, director of consumer Web products, belies her power and influence as a champion of innovation. Mayer has her hands on virtually everything the average Google user sees—from the look of its Web pages to new software for searching your hard drive. And she helps decide which new initiatives get the attention of the company's founders and which don't.

It's no small task. Cofounders Larry E. Page and Sergey Brin have long declared that their mission is to "organize the world's information." Yet only in recent months has the staggering scope of their ambition come into full relief.

Google is moving to digitize the world's libraries, to offer all comers free voice calls, to provide satellite images of the world, and perhaps to give away wireless broadband service to millions of people. Google really seems to believe that it can make every bit of information available to anyone anywhere, and direct

> Google encourages fresh ideas wherever they come from and promotes freewheeling conversations, thus spurring more creative thinking. Employees are able to post their ideas and discuss (or trash) others' on an e-mail list that is circulated throughout the company.

all those bits—whether text, audio, or video—through its computers before they hit users' brains.

Mayer doesn't handle all this herself. One of the key reasons for Google's success is a belief that good ideas can, and should, come from anywhere. Page and Brin insist that all engineers in the company have one day a week to work on their own pet projects. An ideas mailing list is open to anyone at Google who wants to post a proposal. What Mayer does is help figure out how to make sure that good ideas bubble to the surface and get the attention they need. The task is becoming more complex as Google grows, with a workforce of 4,200 now and revenues on track to hit $3.7 billion this year.

> Perhaps one of the biggest enemies of creativity is time—not having enough time to just think, reflect, and work on an idea. At Google, every engineer has one day a week to work on a pet project, even if the project isn't part of the company's mission.

It's increasingly important, too. Google's rocket ride has attracted a swarm of competitors, from giants Microsoft and Yahoo! to upstarts like Technorati and Exalead. They're all aiming to take away a chunk of Google's search traffic, which puts a premium on the company's ability to develop other technologies. "People are used to typing in Google to search," says Chris Sherman, editor of the industry newsletter *SearchDay*. "But its competitors are doing a really good job of rolling out quality features and products." Microsoft Corp. has even explored taking a stake in America Online Inc. so that it can claim for itself the millions in revenues that Google gets from providing AOL with its search technology.

The woman charged with helping to come up with Google's response is a tall, striking blonde with blue eyes. At 30, Mayer still carries herself with the erect posture of the ballet dancer she was in her youth. She grew up in Wausau, Wisconsin, a city of 40,000 about $3^1/_2$ hours northwest of Milwaukee. She aspires to live up to the example of her grandfather, who served as mayor of Jackson, Wisconsin, for 30 years, despite having been crippled by polio as a child.

CHALLENGING CONVENTIONAL WISDOM

In Wausau, Mayer was one of the top debaters on her high school team. Then the brainy teenager decided to try out for the pom-pom squad and made that team, too. To some who knew her, Mayer was making a point. "She wanted to smash the image of the airhead cheerleader," says Jim Briggs, Mayer's high school debate coach. Her debate team ended up winning the Wisconsin state championship; her pom-pom squad was the state runner-up.

A large part of Mayer's success at Google is due to her ability to travel easily between different worlds. When she first joined, the company had something of a high school cliquishness, albeit in reverse. At lunch, the coolest kids—in this forum, the smartest geeks—sat together. On the periphery, sales and marketing folks gathered. Mayer could hold her own in either realm. "She's a geek, but her clothes match," says one former employee.

Mayer continues to bridge the gap between MBAs and Ph.D.s. She helps decide when employees' pet projects are refined enough to be presented to the company's founders. Such decisions are often made through an established process, with Mayer giving ideas a hearing during her open office hours or during brainstorming sessions. Yet she is also good at drawing out programmers informally during a chance meeting in the cafeteria or hallway.

During a casual chat in 2003, a worker told her about the project of an Australian engineer, Steve Lawrence. He was developing a program to track and search the contents of his computer, which ran on the Linux operating system. Knowing that Google had to figure out a way for people to find stuff on their own computers, Mayer tracked Lawrence down and asked him about developing a version of his software to search any PC. He was enthusiastic, so she helped assemble a team to work with him. The result: Google introduced its desktop search in October 2004, two months before Microsoft. "Marissa has been very successful as the gatekeeper for a lot of these new products," says Craig Silverstein, director of technology at Google.

Unlike many large companies, Google doesn't have a this-is-the-way-we-do-it attitude. Executives can recognize when it's time to ditch a company practice or policy.

IF IT'S BROKEN, DITCH IT

Part of Mayer's challenge is realizing when certain formulas are faltering. For years she ran the company's Top 100 priorities list, which ranked projects by order of importance. But as Google's workforce grew, the list soared to more than 270 projects. Last year Google executives decided that the list had run its course and shut it down. "People don't get attached to the processes themselves at Google," says Bret Taylor, product manager for Google Maps. "It's very unusual. Even at small companies, people tend to say: 'This is the way we do X.'"

One of Mayer's strengths is her ability to speak the language of both the geeks and the MBA marketers. As a result, she is able to draw out the computer programmers and engineers and figure out whether their ideas are ready for prime time.

Mayer's typical workday starts at 9 a.m. and doesn't end until about midnight. Her glass-walled office is intentionally situated across from the engineering snack area, where programmers grab evening coffee or munchies. Late at night, engineers will often bend her ear as they take a breather from their work, bringing her up to date on the countless ideas percolating through the ranks. "I keep my ears open. I work at building a reputation for being receptive," she says.

This theory is in action on a sunny Friday afternoon in September. Mayer walks around her office, shared with an assistant and two other employees. Outside the door, seven or eight programmers and product managers have been milling about since 3:30. Most of them are wearing jeans, tennis shoes, and checkered or striped shirts, all untucked. Some pace the hall and talk quietly on their cell phones. Others sit on chairs, their arms folded, waiting patiently.

OPEN DOOR POLICY

At 4 p.m., Mayer's three-times-a-week office hours begin. It's a tradition that Mayer brought over from her days at Stanford, where she taught computer science to undergraduates. Over the years, such meetings have spawned some big ideas, including Google's social-networking site Orkut.

First to enter her office are a pair of techies—a man and woman in their mid-twenties. Sitting across from Mayer, separated by a desk

It's easy to lose the camaraderie and creative energy of a start-up when an organization balloons to more than 4,200 staffers. But Mayer works hard at it, continuing the Google tradition of movie night even though running it has become an administrative nightmare.

with a Dilbert coffee mug and a toy robot still in its box, they forgo the pleasantries and launch into hushed banter. The duo is stumped over which languages the Google Web site should be available in. Although it is already translated into more than 115 tongues, from Arabic to Zulu, they wonder whether they should proceed with more obscure choices. Before one minute elapses, Mayer interjects. Google shouldn't be the arbiter on languages. Just include anything considered legitimate by a third-party source, such as the *CIA World Fact Book*, she says. "We don't want to make a large geopolitical statement by accident."

In ones or twos, all the visitors get a brief hearing, typically five minutes. She gently rebuffs one group that wants to put a link to Hurricane Katrina information on Google's home page. The site for hurricane victims, she argues, isn't useful enough yet. She brainstorms with a product manager on how to measure and compare the freshness of Google's search results against its rivals'.

One of the final groups marches in to discuss a personalized search product. Many pundits describe personalization as the Holy Grail of search. An engine that knows your preferences and interests intimately could tailor the information it delivers and improve results. Google has been offering rudimentary personalization for a year, but more is expected in the future. With two people in Mayer's office and another on speakerphone, she grills the trio about the service's name. She's not enthusiastic about the initial suggestions. "You're killing me," she says.

After a few minutes of discussion, Mayer presses the group on the product's features. Google's top brass is having its

POWER MOVE

To keep Google's design relevant and useful, Mayer frequently puts her employees through different exercises, such as having them create a mock-up of what they think Google will look like in two years. This challenges employees to rethink their assumptions and yields new insights, which can lead to more innovation.

next product-review session shortly, in which nascent ideas get either fast-tracked or sent back for further tinkering. So Mayer asks the big question: "O.K., let's take it to Larry [Page]. Are you guys ready to product-review tomorrow?" They assure her that they're set to go.

CAPTURING IDEAS FROM ANYONE, ANYWHERE

Office hours are just one way in which Mayer connects with inventive engineers and managers. Another is Google's ideas mailing list, the e-mail thread where anyone can submit or comment on an idea. At times, the thread more resembles a form of techie Darwinism. Google newcomers who proffer an especially obvious suggestion ("Why don't we search blogs?") or something off-topic like how to arrange the cafeteria tables often suffer withering rebukes. "It's about 50 percent new ideas, 50 percent indoctrination of new employees," says Mayer.

To make sure that great ideas trickle up, managers have to make themselves approachable. Mayer's glass-walled office is located across from the engineers' snack area, so she can schmooze. She also holds regular office hours to discuss employees' new ideas.

It's all part of a culture that's not for the faint of heart. Google oozes with what one ex-employee calls "geek machismo." Intellectual sparring can get heated. In the cafeteria, "food gets thrown," says the former employee.

FEARLESS CULTURE

What Mayer thinks will be essential for continued innovation is for Google to keep its sense of fearlessness. "I like to launch [products] early and often. That has become my mantra," she says. She mentions Apple Computer and Madonna. "Nobody remembers the Sex Book or the Newton. Consumers remember your average over time. That philosophy frees you from fear."

This is just one way that Mayer tries to maintain the search company's original culture. That's no easy task. Movie night, for instance, was a piece of cake when perhaps 100 employees descended on a local cinema. Today, organizing such an event is a full-time job. Yet Mayer handles several of these a year, from picking a movie with the right geek credibility (say, *Star Wars: Episode III*) to ordering thousands of tickets to writing the software that lets her track who has received them. "She still walks around with a laptop, handing out all the tickets beforehand," marvels Google's Silverstein.

It makes sense for Mayer to stay in such close touch with the swelling ranks of Googlers. She may need every one of their bright ideas to keep the search giant ahead of the competition.

MONDAY MORNING...

THE PROBLEM

Ensuring that employees' breakthrough ideas find their way to top management as the organization's ranks continue to swell

Staying ahead of the competition when rivals are continuing to develop new technology and launch new products

THE SOLUTION

Invite everyone to submit ideas and encourage them to discuss and thrash out ideas, whether through e-mail lists or through exercises.

Give employees the time and freedom to work on developing ideas, even if there doesn't seem to be an immediate payoff.

Stay accessible and keep a friendly, informal atmosphere by organizing casual get-togethers with employees.

SUSTAINING THE WIN

Maintain a culture of fearlessness by launching products early and often, knowing that what's important is the organization's overall record of success, not its occasional failure.

STEVE JOBS:
APPLE'S VISIONARY IS
SHAKING UP DISNEY

Courtesy of Getty Images.

POWER PLAYER

Back in the mid-1990s, Steve Jobs was dismissed as a control freak and prima donna who had made Apple irrelevant. But Jobs remained true to his passion for creating great products and became a leader in the new digital era. Now Jobs steps into the Magic Kingdom.

This February 2006 cover story profile is by Peter Burrows and Ronald Grover with Heather Green.

Create memorable and hip advertising campaigns that will attract consumers and cement the brand's reputation for stylish innovation.

Stay involved in your areas of expertise without micromanaging employees who have the skills that you lack.

Maintain a commitment to creating breakthrough devices of the highest quality, even if that means producing fewer items.

Stay focused on your passion. Staying the course will help you to assemble the kind of talent who are passionate about contributing to something bigger than themselves.

TELL IT LIKE IT IS

Early on a July workday in 1997, Jim McCluney, then head of Apple's worldwide operations, got the call. McCluney was summoned with other top brass of the beleaguered company to Apple Computer Inc.'s boardroom on its Cupertino (California) campus. Embattled Chief Executive Gil Amelio wasted no time. With an air of barely concealed relief, he said: "Well, I'm sad to report that it's time for me to move on. Take care," McCluney recalls. And he left.

A few minutes later, in walked Steve Jobs. The cofounder of the once-proud company had been fired by Apple 12 years before. He had returned seven months earlier as a consultant when Amelio acquired his NeXT Software Inc. And now Jobs was back in charge. Wearing shorts, sneakers, and a few days' growth of beard, Jobs sat down in a swivel chair and spun slowly, says McCluney, currently president of storage provider Emulex Corp. "O.K., tell me what's wrong with this place," Jobs said. After listening to some mumbled replies, he jumped in: "It's the products! So what's wrong with the products?" Again, executives began offering some answers. Jobs cut them off. "The products *suck*!" he roared. "There's no sex in them anymore!"

The one-time *enfant terrible* of the technology world has calmed down considerably en route to becoming a 50-year-old billionaire. But what hasn't changed is his passion for doing, and saying, just about anything to help create the kinds of products that consumers love. In the nine years since Jobs returned to Apple, his unique modus operandi has sparked broad changes in the world of music, movies, and technology.

In the early days of computers, Jobs was considered idealistic for insisting on sleekly designed Apples. But now, as music, movies, and photos are all going digital, consumers are seeking the Apple products.

Now Jobs is stepping into the Magic Kingdom. On January 24, Walt Disney Co. agreed to pay $7.4 billion in stock to acquire Pixar Animation Studios where Jobs is chairman, CEO, and 50.6 percent owner. As part of the deal, Jobs will become the largest shareholder at Disney and will take a seat on the entertainment giant's board. His top creative executive at Pixar, John A. Lasseter, will oversee the movies at both Pixar's and Disney's animation studios.

Pixar's president, Edwin Catmull, will run the business side for the two studios.

BUST THE BOUNDARIES

The alliance between Jobs and Disney is full of promise. If he can bring to Disney the same kind of industry-shaking, boundary-busting energy that has lifted Apple and Pixar sky-high, he could help the staid company become the leading laboratory for media convergence. It's not hard to imagine a day when you could fire up your Apple TV and watch Net-only spin-offs of popular TV shows from Disney's ABC Inc. or use your Apple iPhone to watch Los Angeles Lakers superstar Kobe Bryant's video blog, delivered via Disney's ESPN Inc. "We've been talking about a lot of things," says Jobs. "It's going to be a pretty exciting world looking ahead over the next five years."

One reason for the rich possibilities is that Disney CEO Robert A. Iger is a kindred spirit. The 54-year-old Iger, who succeeded longtime Disney chief Michael D. Eisner on October 1, 2005, is a self-avowed early adopter who listens to a 120-channel Sirius satellite radio in his car. He travels with a pair of iPods, bopping along to the new nano during his 5 a.m. workouts. Jobs seems to know it: Iger says that the first call he got in March, when he was named to the top job, came from the Apple CEO. "He wished me well and hoped we could work together soon," recalled Iger in a 2005 interview.

Lightning fast is more like it. Two weeks after Iger took office, the Disney CEO was on stage at a San Jose movie theater with Jobs as the two men introduced Apple's new video iPod and the availability of such ABC shows as *Lost* and *Desperate Housewives*. The deal came together on Internet time—in just three days. Iger wanted to show that Disney can be a nimble company, willing to embrace the latest digital technologies to deliver its content. "I think we impressed [Jobs and other Apple executives] with how quickly we could make a decision," said Iger in the earlier interview.

Unlike most tech companies, which have had a tin ear when it comes to marketing, Apple has created an image of cool stylishness with its memorable, cutting-edge ad campaigns. Also key: new product launches are kept hush-hush, with the products unveiled by Jobs in dramatic, splashy keynote speeches.

BUILDING ALLIANCES

Yet the alliance has plenty of risks, too. Jobs will have to navigate a minefield of conflicts as he runs Apple and sits on Disney's board. He'll also have to demonstrate that he can take on the unfamiliar role of supporting player. The same perfectionism that allows him to help create great products has made it difficult for him to stand by if someone is going in what he considers to be the wrong direction. When he returned to Apple as part of the NeXT acquisition, he insisted that he didn't want Amelio's job, but then quickly took charge. Already, there's speculation in Silicon Valley that Disney's chief could get "Amelioed."

Iger isn't in the most secure spot. He has revamped Disney's management style and has improved some operations. Still, the company's stock is at about the same level as it was a decade ago. And Iger has been CEO for only a few months, so he's on a new footing with Disney's directors. One management expert calls the Jobs move "courageous" but says, "Iger just put a gun to his head," predicting that Jobs's influence in the boardroom would be so pervasive that Iger could be gone within a year.

Particularly ticklish will be Disney's animation business. While Iger has stressed that it's crucial to the company's future, Jobs may have closer ties, since his two lieutenants will be running the show. Even during the conference call announcing the Disney-Pixar deal, there were hints of differences. One analyst asked whether Lasseter would have the authority to decide whether Pixar movies such as *Toy Story* will be made into Broadway plays. Jobs began by acknowledging that Lasseter works for Iger, then added, "[Lasseter] has always had strong feelings about the exploitation of stories and characters." So if Lasseter and Iger disagree, who will Jobs back?

Jobs declined to be interviewed for this article. But some executives who know him well insist that Iger has nothing to fear. "People are misreading Steve Jobs," says Edgar S. Woolard Jr., the former chairman of Apple and former chairman and CEO of chemical giant DuPont. "If he has a good relationship with you, there is nobody better in the world to work with. Iger made a very wise move, and two years from now everyone will be saying that."

Jobs certainly has much to offer. The past few years have been a thorough vindication of his ideas and leadership. Just a decade ago, he was considered a temperamental micromanager whose insistence on total control and stylish innovation had doomed his company to irrelevance. While Apple tried to develop both the hardware and the software for its computers, Microsoft, Intel, and a flock of PC makers slashed the onetime industry leader to bits by separating the two. Asked in late 1997 what Jobs should do as head of Apple, Dell Inc.'s then-CEO Michael S. Dell said at an investor conference: "I'd shut it down and give the money back to the shareholders."

When a company produces top-quality products, it's usually because the CEO has made it a top priority, as Jobs did. One of his first acts as CEO in 1997 was to chop the product line from dozens of products to just four so as to boost quality.

ABSOLUTE CONTROL, BREAKOUT INNOVATION, STELLAR MARKETING

Those are fighting words that Dell may regret today. Apple shares have soared from $7 a share three years ago to $74, and the company's market cap of $62 billion is just shy of Dell's. Why? Jobs has applied his old strategy to the new digital world. With absolute control, breakout innovation, and stellar marketing, he has created products that consumers lust after. The smooth melding of Apple's iPod with the iTunes software has helped make it an icon of the Digital Age. Rivals from Microsoft to Dell to Sony Corp. have been left in the dust. "He has set the basic model for any digital business from now on," says Toshiba Corp. CEO Atsutoshi Nishida. Microsoft is even considering making its own digital music player, since providing its software to Dell and other hardware developers has failed to slow Apple.

Jobs' success at Pixar is no less remarkable. He bought the business from director George Lucas 20 years ago for $10 million. Catmull and Lasseter believed that they could use computer animation to create full-length movies, even though many in Hollywood and at Disney thought that computers could never deliver the nuance and emotion of hand-drawn animation. Jobs bought into the vision. The result: Pixar has knocked out six blockbusters, from *Toy Story* in 1995 to *Finding Nemo* and *The Incredibles* in recent years. "The great thing about Steve is that he knows that great business comes from great product," says Peter Schneider, the former chairman of Disney's studio. "First you have to get the product right, whether it's the iPod or an animated movie."

FOCUS ON THE KILLER PRODUCT

Many leaders struggle to find a balance between micromanaging and managing. A perfectionist, Jobs has found success by staying involved when it comes to his areas of expertise, but he also steps back when his executives have the know-how that he lacks.

Of course, the trick isn't in wanting to make great products. It's in being able to do it. So what is Jobs's secret? There are many, but it starts with focus and a near-religious faith in his strategy. For years, Jobs plugged away at Apple with his more proprietary approach, not worrying much about Wall Street's complaints. In fact, one of his first moves was to take an ax to Apple's product line, lopping off dozens of products to focus on just four. "Our jaws dropped when we heard that one," recalls former Apple chairman Woolard. Time and again since, Apple has eschewed calls to boost its market share by making lower-end products or expanding into adjacent markets where the company wouldn't be the leader. "I'm as proud of what we don't do as I am of what we do," Jobs often says.

It's all based on a fundamental belief that a killer product will bring killer profits. That's certainly the case at Pixar. While analysts have often urged the company to crank up its movie machine and pump out more releases, the company is only now reaching the point where it can make one a year. And at least until the Disney deal was struck, the plan was to stay at that level for good. The reason: Pixar's executives focus on making sure that there are no "B teams," that every movie gets the best efforts of Pixar's brainy staff of animators, storytellers, and technologists.

Indeed, Jobs says with pride that Pixar has made the tough call to stop production on every one of its movies at some point to fix a problem with a story line or character. "Quality is more important than quantity, and in the end, it's a better financial decision anyway," Jobs told *BusinessWeek* last year. "One home run is much better than two doubles," he said, explaining that then there's only one marketing and production budget rather than two.

The fixation on quality over quantity affects personnel as much as production. Ever since the days when he marveled at Stephen G. Wozniak's engineering skill while building the first Apple computer, Jobs has believed that a small team of top talent can run circles around far larger but less talented groups. He spends a lot of energy working the phones, trying to recruit people he has heard are the best at a certain job.

ENTREPRENEURIAL ENERGY WITHOUT MICROMANAGING

This is one reason that Jobs, while a micromanager at Apple, plays a very different role at Pixar. He handles many of the business duties. But he's very much hands-off on the creative side. Sources say that he typically spends less than one day a week at the company's picturesque campus in Emeryville, across San Francisco Bay from Apple's Cupertino headquarters. "Steve doesn't tell us what to do," says one Pixar employee. "Steve's our benevolent benefactor."

A major reason for Jobs' success is his steadfast, even stubborn belief in his strategy. So he didn't buckle in the early days when Wall Street pressured him to boost market share by making lower-end products.

Jobs may be a multibillionaire, but that hasn't cut into his work ethic. He brings an entrepreneur's energy to tasks that many CEOs would see as beneath them, whether it's personally checking the fine print on partnership agreements or calling reporters late in the evening to talk over a story he thinks is important. And Jobs seems perfectly willing to forgo some aspects of the executive life to focus on his own priorities. For example, unlike most CEOs, he rarely participates in Wall Street analyst conferences.

His famous keynote speeches may be the best example of his intensity. In trademark jeans and mock-turtleneck, Jobs unveils Apple's latest products as if he were a particularly hip and plugged-in friend showing off inventions in your living room. The truth is, the appearance of informality comes only after grueling hours of practice. One retail executive recalls going to a Macworld rehearsal at Jobs's behest, then waiting four hours before Jobs came off the stage to acknowledge his presence. Rude, perhaps, but the keynotes are a competitive weapon. Marissa Mayer, a Google Inc. executive who plays a central role in launching the search giant's innovations, insists that up-and-coming product marketers attend Jobs' keynotes. "Steve Jobs is the best at launching new products," she says. "They have to see how he does it."

Of course, that entrepreneurial zeal is there for a reason: Jobs is one of a shrinking collection of tech chieftains who are actually entrepreneurs. "I was very lucky to have grown up with this industry," Jobs told *BusinessWeek* in 2004. "I did everything coming up— shipping, sales, supply chain, sweeping the floors, buying chips, you name it. I put computers together with my own two hands. As the industry grew up, I kept on doing it."

WHAT CUSTOMERS WANT

In the era of converging media and technology, virtually every company is trying to grow through partnerships. Jobs is choosy about whom he joins forces with; he even walked away from a Pixar deal with Disney because he clashed with then-CEO Michael Eisner.

The same can be said of his role as a movie mogul. Following Pixar's hit with *Toy Story* in 1995, Jobs and then–chief financial officer Lawrence B. Levy gave themselves a crash course in movie business economics. That helped Jobs persuade Disney to agree to a far more lucrative distribution deal than Pixar had had in the past. Former Disney executive Schneider, who negotiated that deal with Jobs, says that he applies equal parts industry knowledge, intensity, and sheer charisma. Jobs prefers to negotiate one-on-one and let lawyers work out the details after the handshake is done. "He says, 'Fine, we have a deal,' and you're saying, 'Wait, wait, I need to check with Michael [Eisner],' and he's saying, 'No, it's done.'"

That's not to say that Jobs is an easy partner. Unlike every other electronics maker, Apple refuses to let even the biggest retailers know what new products are coming until Jobs unveils them. That means that the retailers can't get a jump on arranging ad campaigns or switching out inventory. But Jobs would rather have the surge of publicity that comes with his dramatic product introductions. Indeed, Motorola executives were furious when Apple surprised them by announcing the iPod nano last October, stealing the thunder from the iTunes phone that Apple and Motorola had developed together.

In the final analysis, Jobs' true secret weapon is his ability to meld technical vision with a gut feeling for what regular consumers want and then market the resulting product in ways that make consumers want to be part of tech's cool club. Says a leading tech CEO who requested anonymity: "God usually makes us either left-brain people or right-brain people. Steve seems to have both sides, so he can make extraordinary experiences."

TRANSFERABLE SKILLS

In the wake of the Disney-Pixar deal, the question is how Jobs can apply his unique skills to the media industry. From record labels to music studios, many executives are only reluctantly experimenting with technological change. Besides being concerned that piracy protections aren't strong enough, they're petrified of losing control, since it's unclear how they'll make money in the new world. And Jobs is a polarizing figure. While the major music labels were excited by the possibilities opened up by Apple's iPod, they're now leery that Jobs has pulled a fast one. Apple reaps billions from selling its hit music player, but profits from the songs being sold over the Net are sparse.

The Disney deal may help give Jobs some additional credibility in the media world. While he had a major stake in Pixar in the past, he now sits on the board of one of the biggest media companies in the country. That means that he has a fiduciary responsibility to protect the company's assets, from *Desperate Housewives* to Mickey Mouse.

Iger's assets and Jobs' vision could prove a potent combination. They've already shown that they can experiment in new areas and create enough consumer excitement for others to be compelled to follow. After Iger agreed to put ABC's shows on iTunes for downloading to video iPods, the other major networks followed suit. The same day as the Disney-Pixar agreement, iTunes began offering short films from the early days of Mickey and Goofy. How long before protective movie studio chiefs are digging through back catalogs in hopes of bringing in extra revenues?

Jobs recognizes that he needs great people in order to make a great company. So he invests a lot of time and energy in trying to recruit the best talent.

It's one more way in which iTunes is evolving into something much more powerful than a simple music store. Besides songs, TV shows, and short films, it offers music videos and podcasts from National Public Radio and independents like Brian Ibbott, creator of the cover song show *Coverville*. In December alone, 20 million people visited the site, triple the number for the year before.

What could the future according to Jobs look like? For starters, no radical changes will occur overnight. Given Apple's powerful branding, it's easy to forget that Jobs hasn't typically been the first to pioneer new areas. Many MP3 players existed before the iPod, and Microsoft has been slogging away for years on PCs fit for entertainment in the living room. Apple has taken the first steps in this direction by adding the ability to control a Mac from the couch via the Apple Remote and FrontRow software.

Speculation is rife that Jobs will move Apple fully into the living room, and there's little reason for him not to. The most likely scenario is that Apple will build a version of its Mac mini that can be attached to a TV and entertainment center so that the mini can store family photographs and home videos along with music and videos downloaded from iTunes. Taking this to the extreme, the living room of 2010 may no longer need to have a CD rack, DVD player, TiVo, set-top box, or stereo. All those capabilities could be built into a single box, an Apple TV, or an Apple-branded home entertainment center.

NEW STRATEGIC OPTIONS

Then there's the wireless-phone realm. Apple purchased the domain name iPhone.org years ago and in December trademarked the name Mobile Me. That may suggest that the company will introduce a mobile phone or personal digital assistant to download songs over the air or sync up with a Mac or PC.

The Disney-Pixar deal could open up all sorts of strategic options for Disney and Iger if they can capitalize on Jobs' skills. For example, Disney could decide to push hard toward distributing more of its content directly over the Internet rather than relying on cable companies or movie theaters. Iger has been the most vocal voice in Hollywood on this score of late, even suggesting that new Disney movies should be released on the Internet the same day they hit the cinemas.

Since taking over from Eisner, Iger has shown himself willing to move quickly and take bold steps to remake the bureaucratic company that he inherited. Among Iger's first decisions was to dismantle the corporate strategic planning operation, which Eisner often used to scuttle risky new plans. Iger patched things up with dissident former board members Roy E. Disney and Stanley P. Gold, who had incited a shareholder revolt that kept large investors away. And while Eisner warred with Jobs, Iger worked hard to improve Disney's relationship with him. A key part of the reason for the Disney-Pixar deal, says Jobs, was that "we got to know Bob."

Still, Jobs will be joining a Disney where its old pixie dust is in short supply. As a board member, Jobs may argue for fast-tracking some of the digital distribution experiments that Eisner discarded. Yet that could clash with Iger's ideas about how or how quickly Disney should proceed. A board showdown could prove difficult. Not only is Iger a new CEO, but he also was the second choice among at least some of Disney's 13 board members. (Some favored Meg Whitman, eBay Inc.'s CEO and a former Disney executive.)

Iger's worst nightmare may be that Jobs could sway so many Disney board members that he would win a wide-open race to become Disney chairman. Last year, with the board reportedly split between directors Gary L. Wilson and Robert W. Matschullat, former Senator George J. Mitchell was named interim chairman. He will remain as chairman until he retires at the end of 2006.

Jobs has said that he doesn't want the Disney top board job. Furthermore, that would complicate the potential conflicts of interest with Apple as Disney makes more high-tech deals to distribute its content. Still, the mercurial new Disney board member could make a play to become chairman, say those with knowledge of Disney's board. "The problem then is that Bob would have a larger-than-life chairman to deal with only a year after a larger-than-life CEO was running his life," says one source close to Disney. "I can't imagine he's thrilled over that." Steve Jobs' arrival at the Magic Kingdom could have more thrills than a trip to Disneyland.

THE PROBLEM

Continuing to create innovative products that offer not only functionality but ease of use and a cool design

Making deals and forging winning partnerships that will enable the company to continue to innovate and realize long-term goals

THE STRATEGY

Choose partners carefully, entering into deals only with those who are a good match with the organization, both strategically and temperamentally.

Commit to hiring the best professionals, devoting time and resources to recruiting.

Resist pressure to take shortcuts for short-term gains if it will mean a lowering of standards.

SUSTAINING THE WIN

Relentlessly pursue the organization's vision, staying on course even when there are obstacles and setbacks.

JIM McNERNEY: 3M'S RISING STAR REVS UP INNOVATION

Courtesy of Matthew Gilson

Make the new product development process more efficient by breaking down barriers and encouraging scientists, marketers, and others to work together on new ideas.

Generate new ideas and avoid groupthink by creating a culture in which people feel comfortable debating and speaking their mind, even in front of the chief executive.

Improve the bottom line by setting high goals for managers, while also encouraging them to achieve.

Juice cash flow by cutting costs, improving efficiency, and using savings to troll for acquisitions.

POWER PLAYER

Jim McNerney is the quintessential corporate nomad, changing jobs every two or three years. But both as a top executive at GE and as the CEO of 3M, he has reinvigorated an organization and boosted its growth by giving it rigorous discipline and focus.

This April 2004 story is by Michael Arndt with Diane Brady.

DISCIPLINE, QUALITY, AND FOCUS

Jim McNerney was one of those boys: up early in the morning climbing trees while everybody else in the family was in bed, rousing his three younger brothers to play two-on-two hockey in their basement, running his high school's boys' club, and pitching on the varsity baseball team. And he grew up to be one of those men: for three decades, Walter James McNerney Jr. has climbed the corporate ladder without a pause, uprooting his family every two or three years since earning his master's degree from Harvard Business School in 1975. He job-hopped from Procter & Gamble to McKinsey & Co. and then up through General Electric. On January 1, 2001, after losing a three-way race to succeed John F. Welch as chief executive of GE, he moved on yet again to become chairman and CEO of 3M, the first outsider to head the Saint Paul (Minnesota) company in its century-long history.

It has been a remarkably seamless transition. In many ways, 3M is a mini-General Electric Co. Both are industrial conglomerates that seek to balance slowdowns in one industry with upturns elsewhere, and both have strong traditions of discipline, quality, and an intense focus on measuring and rewarding performance. While both companies have a few world-famous brand names (who doesn't know GE light bulbs or 3M's Scotch tape?), at heart they are bound up with producing the nuts and bolts—as well as the duct tape, turbines, and electronic gear—that keep the industrial world humming.

But 3M had begun to drift. Its vaunted research facilities were turning out fewer and fewer commercial hits, and quarterly results were underwhelming. While 3M still draws many of the world's best chemical engineers, the company's labs haven't had a hit like Post-it Notes since, well, Post-it Notes first came out almost a quarter-century ago. Managers at 3M seemed to know instinctively what they needed, and they found it in McNerney: a strong outsider who could restore discipline and focus. It helped that he started in the midst of a recession, when making painful decisions was easier. After rounds of cost cutting, layoffs, and smart repositioning of the company into more promising fields such as health care, 3M recently announced its best results ever.

Build talent by identifying and nurturing top performers deep in the organization.

Profits have climbed 35 percent since McNerney took over, to $2.4 billion in 2003 on sales of $18.23 billion. 3M's stock price, now just over $81 a share, is also up 35 percent on McNerney's watch, earning it a spot on our most recent BW50 list.

INVENTING THE NEXT BIG THING

That's exactly what you'd expect from a manager schooled in the GE system of rigorous discipline and accountability. But to restore 3M to full health, McNerney needs to do something that his GE background hasn't prepared him for: he needs to return 3M to its historical role as one of Corporate America's most inventive and innovative companies. Over the decades, scientists and engineers in its seven divisions have come up with sandpaper, magnetic audiotape, molds and glues for orthodontia, lime-yellow traffic signs, respirators, floppy disks, Scotch tape, Scotchgard, even a prescription salve for genital warts. To this day, 3M draws its identity from its research might. It devotes $1.1 billion to research every year and has 1,000 scientists and engineers around the world searching for the Next Big Thing.

Going outside and buying innovative outfits, as McNerney has already done, can help, but for his tenure to truly be a success, he needs to coax more out of the company labs. He's trying to do that by redirecting funds into more promising health-care and high-tech research and development, as well as by using Six Sigma, the analytical system made famous at GE, to home in on shortcomings. But it is not at all certain that the creative process that brought Scotchgard fabric protector to the world can flourish under such exacting conditions. In his attempt to determine the commercial potential of ideas early on, McNerney—who has never worked in a lab—might just miss the next Post-it Note.

The flip side to this concern about what McNerney is doing to revitalize 3M is the worry that he won't stay around long enough to finish the job. McNerney, 54, recently celebrated his third anniversary

POWER MOVE

Like so many companies that have lost their inventiveness, 3M was investing heavily in research—some $1 billion a year—that wasn't paying off. McNerney cut funding to projects that weren't yielding results and instead poured money into the fields with the highest potential.

> A leader can't effect lasting change just by demanding it. The staff needs to believe in the mission. To get buy-in, McNerney spent a year soliciting employee input on a new leadership.

with the company, which is about as long as he has held any position in his life. The question is: how many more 3M anniversaries are there in McNerney's future? Given his nomadic past, 3Mers today are whispering anxiously about where their boss is headed next. Nowhere, he swears. McNerney says he has more work to do before 3M is firmly on a high-growth path. He has enrolled a third of 3M's 67,100-person workforce in Six Sigma training, but it has not yet been encoded in the company DNA. He also wants to make 3M much bigger, particularly in fast-growing Asia, perhaps through another acquisition or two. And while he has made management training a priority, establishing 3M's own leadership-development institute, McNerney has no successor ready to take over if he were to leave now. As he says about the challenge of developing potential leaders: "I'm still impressed with how much further we have to go."

He also has personal reasons for staying put. McNerney, who grew up outside Detroit and Chicago, relishes being back in the Midwest after his globe-trotting at GE, say his family and friends. With an extended family around them in the Twin Cities, his three school-age children feel at home. He plays ice hockey with one of his brothers, Peter H. McNerney, in a no-checking league on Sunday evenings. And he can scoot down to Chicago to visit his two adult daughters from his first marriage as well as his parents, who still maintain their home in Chicago's North Shore suburbs. "This is a golden period in Jim's life," says Daniel M. McNerney, another brother, who is now a Presbyterian minister and missionary and lives in Winnetka, Illinois, around the corner from their boyhood home. "He's ambitious, but he's not blindly ambitious. Maybe this is his last job."

COMMAND AND ENCOURAGE

Or maybe it isn't. During the race to run GE, McNerney became known as one of the best managers at one of the best-managed companies in the world. Although he lost the race, his successes at GE and 3M have put him on recruiters' shortlist of most desirable CEOs.

"People come to us and say, 'Go get us a Jim McNerney,'" says Gerard R. Roche, senior chairman of executive recruiters, Heidrick & Struggles International Inc. Indeed, McNerney's name seems to surface whenever a company has a high-profile opening in the offing, whether it's Coca-Cola, Walt Disney, or Merck. As Welch says: "I could see him doing anything."

McNerney's commitment to 3M was severely tested last fall. When Chairman and CEO Philip M. Condit abruptly resigned from Boeing Co., the board is said to have asked McNerney if he would consider the post. He clearly has the credentials: a Boeing director himself, McNerney's last job at GE was running its aircraft-engine unit, one of the aerospace company's main suppliers. The board elevated retired executive Harry C. Stonecipher to CEO instead. But noting that Stonecipher already is 67, some people close to Boeing's directors say that it's only a matter of time before McNerney ends up there.

The secret of McNerney's success is elementary. He sets high goals that can be measured, such as business-unit sales or the rate of product introductions, and demands that his managers meet them. Granted, many CEOs do that today. But like a dedicated teacher or coach, McNerney also works with his team day in, day out, to help them make the grade. "Some people think either you have a demanding, command-and-control management style or you have a nurturing, encouraging style," he says. "I believe you can't have one without the other."

Increasingly, R&D-driven organizations like 3M are prodding their scientists to collaborate with the marketers and manufacturers early on in the new product development process. The reason: it enables them to spot the possible pitfalls and opportunities quickly.

Unusual in this age of celebrity CEOs, and especially for somebody who so far is untouched by scandal or intrigue, McNerney is also one of Corporate America's lowest-profile executives. He has largely ducked the outside world since taking over at 3M. He usually dispatches Chief Financial Officer Patrick D. Campbell to speak for the company, and you can count his national TV appearances on one hand.

His shy-guy public persona is at odds with his image inside the company. There, McNerney is praised as an inspirational leader who is comfortable speaking to big groups or conversing one-on-one. "He's personable," says Charles Reich, executive vice president of 3M's health-care business. "He really engages people." Yet his family and friends say that McNerney genuinely thinks it would be unseemly to draw attention to himself. "It's all about me? No, it's all about my people," says Charles S. Lauer, publisher of *Modern Healthcare* magazine and a neighbor who has known the McNerney family since the 1960s. "That's Jimmy, the captain of the team. He's got his head screwed on straight."

NUMBERS AND POISE

As the first outsider to be named CEO of 3M, McNerney faced a major challenge. But McNerney knows that a key to assimilating to different cultures is to avoid snap judgments. He takes time getting to know the organization and the people.

Sitting at a conference table in his fourteenth-floor office suite, McNerney seems to be enjoying himself. He wears a sports jacket and a polo shirt, his usual work attire. He is quick to attribute 3M's achievements to the entire organization and praises 3Mers for their work ethic. "My experience is that if people are convinced they're growing as they pursue company goals, that's when you get ignition," he says. He is also disciplined and direct; he makes his points and doesn't utter a word more. When the allotted time for the appointment ends, he stands up and retreats to his inner office. Back to work.

McNerney inherited his character—and perhaps his wanderlust—from his dad, say his family and friends. After a stint in hospital management in Providence, Rhode Island, where Jim was born, Walter J. McNerney Sr. was a health-policy professor at three universities, as well as president of the Blue Cross & Blue Shield Assn. in Chicago. Walter and Shirley, a homemaker, pushed their daughter and four sons hard: all of them except Dan hold graduate degrees in business. But even as Walter gained national recognition, he always maintained his humility and insisted that his children do the same. "If any of us was ever tooting our own horn, Dad would let us have it," recalls Dan. "Pride was a terrible thing."

Although academic achievement was always number one in the McNerney household, sports came a close second. Jim played baseball and hockey—and lost a few teeth on the ice—while getting his bachelor's degree in American Studies at Yale University, his father's alma mater. "He was certainly never a hot dog," says his brother Pete, managing partner of Thomas, McNerney & Partners, a venture-capital firm in Minneapolis that specializes in health-care start-ups. "He was a guy you depended on. It's no surprise to me that he's running something big."

At first, though, it was slow going. McNerney's career started anonymously enough in 1975 as a brand manager for the Downy fabric-softener account at Procter & Gamble Co. He was assigned to two other accounts, Coast and Bounce, before he left in 1978 to become a senior manager with consulting firm McKinsey in Chicago.

His ascent quickened after he was hired three years later by GE as a vice president in its information-services department. In less than a decade, he was promoted four times, reaching the ranks of upper management in 1991 as president and CEO of GE's electrical distribution and control unit. He was 42. Welch recalls McNerney catching his attention early on. What made him stand out? His knack for numbers and his poise, Welch says. "He was just able to handle himself perfectly, even though he was very young."

McNerney really impressed the boss, though, when he was dispatched to Hong Kong as president of GE's Asia-Pacific business in 1993. At the time, the Fairfield (Connecticut) giant had no operations of its own in China and was desperate to enter what has since become a $3 billion market for the company. McNerney established its first wholly owned unit within two years and then began staffing the operation before leaving in 1995.

TEAM FOCUS

But the job that gave him a shot at taking over from Welch was yet to come. In 1997, after two years as chief of GE's lighting unit, based in Cleveland, McNerney was yanked back to Cincinnati to head GE Aircraft Engines. Welch admits today that even he had some doubts about how his protégé would do. The aircraft industry is notoriously insular, distrustful of anyone

One secret of McNerney's success as a leader is that he remains focused on the team and always shares credit. Even as CEO, he is happy to focus on managing, letting others share the limelight.

who never wore "a scarf and goggles," as Welch puts it. Yet McNerney bested the insiders. When he arrived at GE Aircraft Engines, it was a distant third-place supplier to Boeing for its twin-engine 777 planes. But in 1999, he cinched a deal making the unit the exclusive engine supplier for Boeing's new long-range 777 aircraft. The 20-year contract was valued at more than $25 billion.

OUTHUSTLING RIVALS

McNerney did it by outhustling his rivals. He became a frequent flier to Seattle, then Boeing's headquarters, to find out what was keeping Boeing from doing business solely with GE. Executives there were concerned that airlines that had never serviced GE engines before wouldn't want to take on such a risk. So McNerney called the heads of Singapore Airlines, Cathay Pacific Airways, and others and got them on board by promising that GE would do everything it could to help them maintain the engines. He used GE's leverage, too. The company's aircraft-leasing unit pledged to buy the planes from Boeing and then lease them to airlines—if GE got an exclusive deal. And he enlisted Welch to personally lobby Boeing's Condit.

In the end, of course, that success wasn't enough. On a rainy day in late November 2000, Welch flew to Cincinnati and met privately with McNerney in an airplane hangar to deliver the news: he had picked Jeffrey R. Immelt, the head of GE Medical Systems and the front-runner all along in the succession race, to be the next CEO. Immelt's edge: he was six years younger than either McNerney or the other finalist, Robert L. Nardelli, now chairman and CEO of Home Depot Inc. Immelt was also judged to be more at ease in the spotlight. "You chose the wrong guy," a disappointed McNerney told Welch. But he didn't press the point. He didn't need to.

Even as Welch was still mulling his personnel options, McNerney's name had been passed along to 3M directors by headhunter Roche at Heidrick & Struggles. That spring, 3M's directors had decided to go outside for a chairman and CEO to replace Livio "Desi" DeSimone, who had announced that he planned to retire by year-end. An engineer and lifelong 3Mer who took over as CEO in 1991, DeSimone had been unable to keep the company's storied history of innovation alive. Growth rates for sales stalled while profits yo-yoed. The company's share price peaked in mid-1997, then drifted lower even as the overall market raced ahead. "We needed to jump-start the company," recalls

Edward A. Brennan, a former chairman and CEO of Sears, Roebuck & Co. who chaired 3M's CEO search committee. "We sensed that Jim would be a perfect agent for change."

Given the chilly reception that some "change agents" face, McNerney was braced for a tough time—especially since he not only was the first CEO who hadn't come up through the 3M ranks, but wasn't even an engineer. But he says employees generally encouraged him to shake things up. "I found a company who thought they weren't achieving all they could, and they were willing to team up with somebody to do more," he says. "That was a surprise." It helped that 3M and GE were so similar. It also helped that McNerney was used to contending with different corporate cultures.

Oddly, the deepening manufacturing recession helped, too. In September 2000, hosting his last biennial conference for analysts and investors, DeSimone forecast an 11 percent increase in revenue in the year ahead and a 12 percent rise in operating income. 3M's telecommunications business would do even better, he predicted, with sales and profits surging 25 percent as customers strung more and more fiber-optic lines. But by 2001's first quarter, operating earnings were crumbling in every business except consumer and office products. The abrupt downturn proved that things had gone awry and gave McNerney latitude to move even faster. All at once, he notes, "we were all in this together." Quickly, and with little dissent, he ordered a cut of 5,000, or 6.6 percent, in the company's workforce.

INVEST IN GROWTH

Although less apparent, other, more fundamental changes followed. Under McNerney's predecessors, 3M had always been an egalitarian operation. Every year, each business got the same bump in its budget, no matter how it had performed. No longer. McNerney and his executive team began allocating R&D and marketing funds according to the growth potential of each business. That meant more for health care, now 3M's biggest business, with $4 billion in sales and $1 billion in operating earnings, and its display and graphics business, which boasted a 66 percent surge in 2003 operating profits thanks to the ultrathin plastic films it makes for flat-screen TVs and mobile phones. But it also meant less for everyone else, particularly 3M's old-line industrial and transportation businesses.

McNerney is also targeting where in the world 3M spends its money, shifting more resources and personnel out of the United States, where growth is slower and costs are higher, and into China and other red-hot markets in Asia. Because of targeted layoffs and attrition, last year U.S. staff fell by an additional 1,700, to 33,300, helping to reduce 3M's total payroll by 10 percent since McNerney took over. Meanwhile, 3M's headcount in Asia rose 5 percent, to 9,900. Capital spending in the United States also dropped in 2003, to $425 million, and has been reduced by one-third over the past three years. In Asia, capital expenditures have increased 25 percent, to $102 million in the past year. The migration, moreover, isn't just in manual labor; 3M is moving R&D and product design to China as well. McNerney admits that the domestic downsizing hurts the U.S. economy but says he must proceed. "I'm responsible for keeping 3M a globally competitive company," he says. "Now, it's very hard to serve Chinese customers in a lot of our businesses unless we're manufacturing there. We don't do this to eviscerate U.S. jobs. We do it to be competitive."

> Achieving breakthrough ideas requires welcoming open discussion— and dissent. McNerney spent much of his time talking and listening to 3M employees, showing that he was serious about promoting dialogue.

TARGETED INNOVATION

What McNerney hopes will be his true legacy at 3M, though, is to restore the company to its glory days as one of America's preeminent idea factories, a place where cutting-edge research results in groundbreaking new products. So, borrowing again from the GE way, McNerney has acquired new products to pump up 3M's growth rate. In late 2002, 3M paid $850 million for Corning Precision Lens Inc., instantly giving it a big presence in the rear-projection TV market and complementing its other TV component businesses.

His real emphasis, however, is on what the company can do for itself. McNerney now has his scientists talking with the marketing and manufacturing folks right from the start to steer lab work in more profitable directions. For example, sales reps polled TV makers to see what they wanted next in flat-screen models. The response: a wider viewing area, so that people don't have to sit squarely in front of the screen, and a deeper black in the background color. Now researchers are tinkering with optic films to achieve those attributes.

The new way has its own risks, however. In the past, 3M researchers had the leeway to spend 15 percent of their time on pet projects. This officially sanctioned moonlighting has paid off for 3M big time. Its Aldara salve—an immune-response modifier just approved to treat precancerous skin conditions—was discovered by a scientist who kept experimenting with the drug. Post-it Notes, too, was another brainchild of scientists who tinkered for years, ignoring the naysayers in manufacturing and marketing. Now these researchers are being reined in. Won't they object? Not likely, says James B. Stake, executive vice president of 3M's display and graphics business. As the inventor of a few gadgets that never amounted to anything, he argues that today's setup will increase the odds of success. "We'll find many fewer individuals going down blind alleys," he says. True, but some worry that by micromanaging the labs, 3M could miss breakthrough ideas in unexpected places.

McNerney is also bringing more management rigor to 3M through Six Sigma. Originally a form of statistical analysis used to reduce product error, at GE in the 1990s it morphed into a companywide tool for cost cutting. Specially trained "black belts" are now doing the same thing at 3M, and then some. They're using Six Sigma for everything from sharpening sales pitches to developing new kinds of duct tape. McNerney says that Six Sigma also turns out to be a low-risk way to spot up-and-coming managers because it provides straightforward measurements of their performance. So far, a quarter of the 1,000 3M employees who have completed Six Sigma have been promoted two steps or more.

Today, McNerney figures that he spends most of his time on personnel. Every other week, he addresses groups of employees at company headquarters. He begins the two-hour sessions with an update on 3M's numbers and a progress report on Six Sigma and his other initiatives. Then, for the last hour and a half, he takes questions. He does the same thing when he visits 3M's far-flung facilities around the world. McNerney also is a regular instructor at 3M's leadership-development institute, another program he has borrowed from GE. In between, he monitors how members of his operating committee— 3M's top 15 executives—are doing, often swinging by their offices for a chat. If a manager isn't measuring up, McNerney probably won't raise his voice. But he will expect a solution, pronto. "I think all of us are working harder than we've ever worked before," says David W. Powell, 3M's senior vice president of marketing.

Powell should know: among the top ranks, he is one of the few holdovers from the DeSimone era. Only two of 3M's seven business heads were at their posts under the previous CEO. But there was no purge. Instead, the departing executives left one by one as they neared 3M's mandatory retirement age of 65, only to be replaced by other 3Mers. There are just two outsiders in McNerney's inner circle: CFO Campbell, who came from General Motors Corp., and General Counsel Richard Ziegler, a former partner at Cleary, Gottlieb, Steen & Hamilton in New York, who had been McNerney's classmate at Yale.

When McNerney isn't overseeing his managers, he is tending to 3M's customers. In January, W.W. Grainger Inc., a $4.7 billion industrial-goods wholesaler that carries 1,300 3M products, got the McNerney treatment—honed, needless to say, at GE. As executives at the Lake Forest (Illinois) company went over sales trends with their top suppliers, McNerney listened in. Then he met separately with the company's chief operating officer. In all, McNerney spent some three hours at Grainger. And while 3M had regularly sent someone to visit the company, that someone had never been the CEO. "It was a significant event," says Michael A. Pulick, vice president for product management. "3M is truly trying to get to know our business."

> While many managers think that they have to choose between being commanding and being nurturing, McNerney achieves results by striking a balance between the two. The harder you push people, he says, the more you have to encourage them.

MEASURES OF SUCCESS

McNerney's efforts are clearly paying off. In 2003, sales rose in every one of 3M's businesses except telecom, while operating income was up in all but industrial. Cash flow swelled by 29 percent, to $3.79 billion, and the company's operating margin widened by a full percentage point, to 20.9 percent. His goal is to boost sales by at least 5 percent a year, excluding acquisitions, and profits by 11 percent or more annually. 3M was slated to beat both targets in 2004, with sales up 6.5 percent and profits growing 16.5 percent, says McNerney.

Analyst John G. Inch of Merrill Lynch & Co. predicted that the company would be able to exceed its targets again in 2005, with earnings nearing $3.3 billion.

Success seems to be agreeing with McNerney. Family and friends say that despite the pressure of being boss, McNerney seems more relaxed today than he has been in years. He and his wife, Haity (they met at a GE gym that she had set up for the company), both work out and run regularly. McNerney also occasionally skips business dinners to coach his son's ice hockey team. He skis, golfs, and every May sails on Chesapeake Bay with his brothers and business chums. And he and the family like to jet off to Montana, where he owns a home in a mountain resort.

So is this the last stop for McNerney? If it were, he would be going out on top, in charge of one of the nation's most venerable companies. How many other jobs could give him that satisfaction? Certainly McNerney doesn't need the money. He received $4.9 million in salary and bonus in 2003 and options worth $5.8 million, raising the value of his 3M options to $67.7 million. He also holds $15 million in restricted stock. "It feels like home here," he says. "I'm a 3Mer." Still, he won't turn 65 until 2014. And recruiters are tempting him with job offers all the time. "We're professional movers," he acknowledges. "I could pitch a tent anywhere." He is still one of those boys.

MONDAY MORNING...

MONDAY

THE PROBLEM

Restoring a company once known for great ideas to its former glory

Persuading a tradition-bound organization to make big changes when the leader is an outsider

THE STRATEGY

Focus R&D resources in the high-growth areas, while also trolling outside the organization for new, promising companies to buy.

Resist the temptation to rush to judgment, taking time to get to know the players and the culture.

Win buy-in by involving employees in a dialogue about the future of the company.

SUSTAINING THE WIN

Lead by example and inspire employees to perform at the highest level by being generous with praise and remaining focused on the work.

RUSSELL SIMMONS: FROM HIP-HOP TO MAINSTREAM

© Henry Leutwyler

Create a brand identity that remains true to its hip-hop roots, even while launching new businesses and striking deals with corporate America.

Market products with "urban cool" to mainstream and suburban consumers without alienating your base.

Turn the head of the company into an icon, an arbiter of style.

POWER PLAYER

With a clothing line, a music label, TV shows, a credit card, and even an energy drink, Russell Simmons is fast expanding his hip-hop empire. The key: he is partnering with stodgy corporations— without losing his edgy style.

Russell Simmons has brought urban style to mainstream America. This 2003 article by Susan Berfield, with Diane Brady and Tom Lowry, offers an inside look at his growing influence.

HIP-HOP IN CORPORATE AMERICA

Russell Simmons lives in Corporate America, but not quite of it. The impresario of hip-hop, self-made 46-year-old entrepreneur has started two of the most successful enterprises of their kind: the hip-hop music label Def Jam and the clothing line Phat Farm. Simmons, more than anyone else, has helped bring an urban sensibility, with its bravado, exaggerated desires, and urgent longing for the good life, to popular culture. It's the Nu American Dream.

Phat Farm, a $263 million company, sells itself as "classic American flava with a twist"; its logo is an upside-down American flag. One of Simmons' new clothing lines, Run Athletics, is featured in Sears Roebuck & Co. and J. C. Penney Co. Another, Def Jam University, will be available in Sears next year; it alone could be worth $100 million before the end of the decade. Already, Phat Farm does its best business in a chain of stores called d.e.m.o., located almost entirely in suburban malls. The word *phat* ("highly attractive or gratifying") has been added to the Merriam-Webster Collegiate Dictionary.

Hardly a major consumer company around isn't trying to cash in on hip-hop's singular popularity, if not its edgy authenticity. Hip-hop music and its signature style, rap, emerged from mostly impoverished, largely African American urban neighborhoods and today dominates youth culture. It's not about race or place. It's an attitude, a state of mind. Marketing experts estimate that one-quarter of all discretionary spending in America today is influenced by hip-hop. Coke, Pepsi, Heineken, Courvoisier, McDonald's, Motorola, Gap, Cover Girl, and even milk: all use hip-hop to sell themselves. "There has been a bona fide cultural shift," says Marian Salzman, chief strategic officer at advertising agency Euro RSCG Worldwide. "This is the new mainstream," says Erin Patton, president of the Mastermind Group, marketing consultants. And, in truth, there is no easy way to fully calculate hip-hop's impact on our clothes, our cars, our movies, our music, our commercials, and our very language.

FLUID AND FRUGAL

Simmons is what you might call an extreme entrepreneur, and he has created a new kind of empire, one that is organic (he operates more on instinct than anything else), fluid (businesses come and go), and frugal (he usually doesn't risk much of his own money). In some ways, the company's name—Rush Communications Inc.—says it all. Rush, which was Simmons's childhood nickname, sums up the defiant, impatient, hungry stance that is hip-hop. "Any company that wants to tap into the youth market today has to pay attention to Russell," says Frank Cooper, the head of multicultural market development at Pepsi. "He is one of the principal architects of hip-hop culture. It's a market that is massive and that is global."

Simmons prefers to call himself a pioneer, and a generation of young, brash entrepreneurs has come to regard him as such. "Here's what other people's business plan is: let Russell bash his head," he jokes, "and then we'll follow." Rush Communications has ventured into nearly every haunt of popular culture. Phat Farm has grown to include a women's line called Baby Phat as well as children's clothes, sneakers, and accessories. The entertainment group has produced two popular programs for HBO and a Tony Award–winning Broadway show. This year Simmons introduced the Rush Visa Card, a prepaid debit card for people who may or may not have a bank account. There's even a vitamin-fortified energy drink, DefCon3, that is now selling in 5,000 7-Eleven stores around the country.

Over the years, Simmons has also opened and closed an advertising agency, developed and sold a Web site, launched a bimonthly magazine, and discarded the idea of creating a chain of fast-food vegan restaurants (he long ago gave up eating "anything that runs away from me"). He has started the Rush Philanthropic Arts Foundation, which gave away about $350,000 last year to groups that introduce underprivileged kids to the arts, and the Hip-Hop Summit Action Network, which tries to persuade teenagers to become involved in politics.

Simmons himself has found favor with some of the most straitlaced companies around. He was the first person to design a series of limited-edition Motorola Inc. cell phones with his name on them. His wife, Kimora Lee Simmons, a 27-year-old former model who started the Baby Phat women's line three years ago, was the second.

With roughly one-quarter of all discretionary spending today believed to be influenced by hip-hop culture, the blue chips are increasingly eager to tap this new market. Simmons is profiting from their need, growing his company by making deals with establishment companies, from Motorola to Sears.

He also advises Motorola on how to insinuate itself further into the hip-hop community, where a cell phone has become a fashion statement. As Tamara S. Franklin, the director of strategic planning and new business development for Motorola's iDEN subscriber group, puts it, "We want to intertwine our brands."

Simmons struck a marketing agreement with Grimoldi, an Italian luxury watchmaker, as it was first entering the United States, largely on the basis of a single phone call he made to introduce the company's young chief executive to Donald Trump. Simmons and Trump might seem an unlikely pair, but they've been friends for years. "Russell has a great ability to see where the world is going and to take advantage of it," Trump says. These days, Simmons, who invested in Grimoldi, features the oval-shaped watches in Phat Farm ads, hands out the $1,800-plus pieces to everyone from Arnold Schwarzenegger to Nike's $90 million man, LeBron James, and offers design suggestions (yellow bands for summer and, always, more diamonds).

POWER MOVE

Like many wildly successful entrepreneurs, Simmons generates lots of ideas and will experiment. But he isn't married to his ideas and will discard what doesn't work. In recent years, for instance, he has killed his plan to create a chain of vegan restaurants and sold an ad agency that he launched.

Recently, PepsiCo, the company that Simmons once threatened to boycott after it dropped Def Jam artist Ludacris as a spokesman, has taken an interest in DefCon3. "Our goal in 2004 is to become much more ingrained in the lifestyle of the hip-hop community," says Cooper. General Motors Corp. is even considering putting out a Russell Simmons Yukon Denali. "He's an icon," says Chris Robinson, the director of diversity sales and marketing at GM. "What he touches usually turns to gold."

ULTIMATE STATUS SYMBOL

For these companies, Simmons is a guide to an unfamiliar world, one that can be coarse, raw, and violent. The songs, Simmons says, are real, if uncomfortable, expressions of life on the streets. In the mid-1990s, two of the most popular rappers around, Tupac Shakur and the Notorious B.I.G., were murdered. Others have lived perilously close to disaster: Beanie Sigel, a convicted felon whose clothing line is called State Property, is facing trial for gun possession; Jay-Z, who has designed a collection of Reebok sneakers, was a former crack dealer; 50 Cent, who soon will have his own line of sneakers too, boasts of having been shot nine times. About which Micky Pant, Reebok's chief marketing officer, says, "They were brought up under extraordinarily difficult circumstances. We judge people by their actions now." There are many good reasons for this tolerance. One is that when Reebok launched the limited-edition $100 S. Carter shoe (Jay-Z's real name is Shawn Carter) on Easter weekend, it sold faster than any shoe in Reebok's history. The next day, says Pant, the S dot, as it's called, was going for $250 a pair on eBay.

The seamy side of hip-hop is what makes Simmons so valuable to mainstream marketers who want to adopt what's fresh about hip-hop without appearing to condone what's dangerous. They trust Simmons to navigate the fine line between edgy and appalling, authentic and offensive. Or, as Antonio Piredda, the 35-year-old head of Grimoldi, says: "I know that Russell can figure out what is good and what is not."

For Simmons, as much as for the artists, these deals are the ultimate status symbol, a sign that hip-hop can feed off the corporate world and not just the other way around. "To us it's not selling out," he says. "We want what represents success."

Simmons is in some ways the perfect twenty-first-century company man: a celebrated executive who unashamedly promotes his products and his political concerns, often at the same time. At some 25 store appearances this year, during dozens of television and radio interviews, at the regular talks he has with school kids in his Manhattan office, at his hip-hop summits around the country, at his annual Hamptons fund-raiser for his foundation, and, this spring, at the rallies he sponsored to protest New York State's harsh penalties for nonviolent drug crimes, Simmons never, ever mentions one without the other. The ads for a new line of sneakers include calls for reparations for African Americans, and the label on DefCon3 says: "Energize yourself and empower your community by drinking a healthier smart energy soda that gives back." He says that a portion of sales from both the sneakers and the soda will go to the cause.

"MISUNDERESTIMATED"

Yet when it comes to assessing the relationship between his hip-hop nation and Corporate America, Simmons is decidedly ambivalent.

To keep his image of urban cool, Simmons knows that he has to keep his street credibility. One way he does that is by proudly using his brand to promote political causes (and vice versa). So the ads for his line of sneakers include calls for reparations for African Americans, and he says that a portion of sales goes to the cause.

He has seen up close how some companies try to take advantage of the urban community's ability to detect and set cultural trends without bankrolling its entrepreneurs, yet he has benefited greatly from not being taken seriously at first, from being "misunderestimated," as it were. "I could complain about the lack of cultural sensitivity," he says, "but I also say that because of the old guys' stupidity I'm here in the first place. If the music business understood hip-hop in the beginning, I wouldn't have built Def Jam. If Hollywood knew about Chris Rock, I wouldn't have had *Def Comedy Jam* [an HBO show]. If the banks served these folks, I wouldn't be here with the Rush Card. I wouldn't be here without their arrogance."

"Here" in this case is an extravagantly maintained $14 million estate in suburban New Jersey that he bought two years ago for his wife, who eagerly mentions that it is among the biggest homes on the East Coast. It includes an indoor pool, a movie theater, a gym, 11 bedrooms, furniture that Gianni Versace once owned, several Swarovski crystal chandeliers, and at least one six-figure Egyptian vase. His touches include a photograph of Louis Farrakhan hanging in the dining room and, in the foyer, an old sign that says "Waiting Room for Colored People." In the garage are Kimora Lee's Bentley, which she's about to trade in for an extra-long Maybach, and what Simmons calls his Osama-mobile, a Ford Expedition with a 500-channel TV.

On a July afternoon, Simmons sits on a yellow brocade couch in his living room, legs folded under him, his signature cell phone, a Motorola two-way, and a can of DefCon3 at hand. He is wearing what he always wears: Phat Farm's preppy, baggy clothes, a baseball cap, and white sneakers. This is a crucial time for Simmons. After 11 years of going it alone, he's hoping to sell Phat Farm to one of the big apparel companies for a couple of hundred million dollars so that he can "amp up" and devote more of his time to designing and marketing the clothing line. Simmons wants Phat Farm to be a multibillion-dollar business, the next Polo Ralph Lauren, and only

a corporation with serious resources can
knows that the allure of rap will inevitably
year, sales of rap music have actually fallen
hip-hop empire is bigger than that, but still,
it is safely ensconced in the Establishment.

Simmons generally says what's on his mind
an energetic 54-year-old fashion veteran who is
Farm, has counseled that he's better off not naming   . So he
continues: "There's been a lack of vision on the part of major clothing
companies. We've been overlooked." Nothing infuriates Simmons
more than someone dismissing Phat Farm as an ethnic label. Urban
wear, as it's called, is a $2 billion business, according to Marshal
Cohen, an analyst at NPD Group. It's the fastest-growing segment
in an otherwise dreary fashion industry, and it is sold around the
country, often to white, suburban teenagers. It ranges from Phat
Farm's casual chic to Sean Jean's more flamboyant men's wear (put
out by hip-hop executive and J. Lo-ex P. Diddy). "As a retailer, you'd be
blacklisted by consumers if you don't have an urban line," says Cohen.
Derrick Flowers, senior buyer for young men's wear at J. C. Penney,
says that hip-hop labels account for half of all sales in his department.

By mid-August, Simmons is more hopeful. Ruby Azrak is a
boisterous, fast-talking Brooklyn native who holds a stake in Phat
Farm and serves as Simmons's alter ego in
the business world. He also oversees the
licenses for the company and has just
worked out a deal with Kellwood Co.,
a $2.6 billion clothing maker, to put out the
more modestly priced Def Jam University.
Hal J. Upbin, the head of Kellwood,
says of his partnership with Simmons:
"At first I wasn't sure what to expect.
But I became increasingly comfortable with
what he stands for in the hip-hop
community. We would like to evolve our
relationship further."

Simmons is sitting in his office, which is
located in Manhattan's fashion district but
looks for all the world like a men's club, with

Instead of holding a grudge against corporate America for dismissing African American culture and failing to bankroll its entrepreneurs, Simmons saw and seized the market opportunities. "I could complain about the lack of cultural sensitivity," he says, "but . . . [it's] because of the old guys' stupidity I'm here in the first place."

MARKETING POWER PLA

151

-paneled walls, leather couch, and Oriental rug. Though ices yoga daily and meditates in front of a shrine that udes a statue of the Hindu goddess of wealth, Laxmi, serene he is not. Simmons is hyperkinetic, uneasy with lulls, an executive whose stance is simple: bring it on. And now that he's on the verge of making the biggest deal of his life, he can't stop talking about it, even though Corbett and Azrak are signaling him to stay quiet. "You know how Wall Street wants public companies to grow?" he says. "Well, the street wants us to grow. The street is watching. The hip-hop community takes pride in growth. They love big. Not cool, small, and alternative. Hip-hop aspires to own the mainstream."

That ambition is key to understanding hip-hop's new generation of streetwise, swaggering entrepreneurs, educated, as they say, in the school of hard knocks. Indeed, almost everyone connected to hip-hop seems to have an incipient business venture or two on the side. Kevin Leong, the 25-year-old head of design at Phat Farm, has his own company, Black Bean Sauce; he created pouches for Simmons' Motorola phones. As David Mays, the 34-year-old Harvard-educated cofounder of the hip-hop magazine *The Source*, says:

Simmons believes that doing big business with corporate giants isn't "selling out." The reason: he gets straitlaced companies to *buy in* to hip-hop, rather than the other way around, so that his brand isn't diluted.

"People want to start their own businesses and think they can. It's one of the staples of our culture." Damon Dash, for example, is a 32-year-old producer who, with Jay-Z, runs Roc-a-Fella Enterprises, which at last count included a clothing line, a music label, a moviemaking enterprise, and a brand of vodka, Armadale. He states the hip-hop ethos with a certain crass elegance: "People exploit us, and we exploit them back. If they're going to make a buck off us, we'll make a buck off them. That's just the way it's going to be." This, for the lucky ones, is the Nu American Dream.

STRAIGHT OUT OF HOLLIS

Russell Simmons started out as a small-time hustler in the middle-class neighborhood of Hollis, in Queens, New York. He was raised by parents who had both graduated from college: his father worked for the board of education, his mother for the city recreation department. As a teenager, Simmons ran with the local hoodlums; he sometimes dealt drugs, and he mostly spent the money on clothes.

He enrolled in the City College of New York in 1975, at a time when hip-hop was just emerging from the streets of Queens and Harlem. He had an immediate entrée right into the center of it all: his younger brother, Joey, was a rapper whose group, Run-DMC, was starting to get some attention. Russell, always enterprising, became the group's manager, then took on other groups; he dropped out of school just short of graduation and eventually cofounded Def Jam with another promoter, Rick Rubin, a New York University undergrad from Long Island.

LIVING LARGE

Over the next decade, as hip-hop's influence spread, Russell and Joey, or Run, as he is known, lived large: They toured the world, took drugs, dated models. In those early years, though, hip-hop was still largely ignored by the major record companies. "We were left alone to incubate ourselves," says Lyor Cohen, who was born to Israeli parents, raised in Los Angeles, and started working with the Simmons brothers in the early 1980s. By 1985, hip-hop's popularity could no longer be brushed aside; Sony Corp. signed a distribution deal with Def Jam. (When the company eventually was bought by Universal Music, it was combined with a rock-and-pop label to become Island Def Jam.) Throughout this time, Cohen managed the business, with varying degrees of involvement by Simmons. Now the label, last year the industry's second largest, with sales of more than $700 million, is run solely by Cohen.

By the mid-1980s, the strangely alluring, sometimes lopsided relationship between hip-hop and the business world had begun. Run-DMC came out with a song about Adidas sneakers in 1986 and ended up with a million-dollar endorsement contract. "We weren't trying to sell Adidas at first. I wrote a song about what was in my life. We were doing what we loved, and the money followed," says Reverend Run (he was ordained by Zoe Ministries Community Congregation in New York in 1994). Now, in a fitting reprise, he is in charge of Phat Farm Footwear.

Since those more innocent days, marketers and rappers alike have set about to exploit that potential much more systematically.

When Barbara Jackson, a vice president of marketing at Allied Domecq, the company that sells Courvoisier, wanted to introduce the cognac to the hip-hop community, she turned to Simmons' advertising agency, dRush, for help. And what do you know? In the summer of 2002, popular rappers Busta Rhymes and P. Diddy (also known as Puff Daddy) put out a song called "Pass the Courvoisier" with a chorus that included the lines: "Give me some money, you can give me some cars. You can give me the bitch, but make sure you pass the Courvoisier." Jackson describes her reaction: "As a marketer, you're thrilled. You can't buy this. Well, you could, but it's more credible when you don't have to." Sales of the venerable cognac spiked 20 percent that year. Courvoisier didn't pay Busta Rhymes for the song. It never signed a contract with him. It did sponsor grand parties after his concerts.

ENTERING THE FASHION WORLD

Simmons, of course, has been trading on his name ever since he launched Phat Farm in 1992. Back then, Tommy Hilfiger Inc.'s clothes had become the uniform of choice on the street, and the black-owned FUBU (For Us By Us) was starting to establish itself. Simmons figured that there would be interest in an alternative if it came from him, and he began putting together the pieces of a fashion company, all the while jetting back and forth to Hollywood, where he and Brian Grazer produced *The Nutty Professor*. Then he discovered yoga and met Kimora Lee, and both began to take hold of him. He gave up drinking, gave up smoking, gave up meat, and gave up fur (much to Kimora Lee's dismay). And in 1998, he approached Ruby Azrak, who had been in the men's underwear business for three decades and whom he knew from New York fashion shows, for advice on how to run Phat Farm. "He was an absentee owner in the apparel business, and you can get destroyed that way," says Azrak. "He was looking for me to guide him."

Azrak's first suggestion was to get out of the manufacturing business and go into licensing instead. Two weeks later they closed a $75 million licensing deal on a handshake. "I knew his word was fabulous," says Azrak. "That's the way he runs his life. He doesn't walk around with a posse, or bodyguards. He's not on an ego trip." Soon Azrak, a Syrian Jew who lives on the same Brooklyn street where he was born and keeps a Hebrew prayer on his office wall, took a stake in what was then about a $15 million company. Now the apparel business is nearly 20 times that size, and he, Lyor Cohen, and another investor that they decline to identify own 40 percent of it; Russell and Kimora Lee own the rest. Azrak describes his role this way: "I do the business deals, but once the contract is signed, then everything goes to Russell. He approves all the designs, the samples, the marketing. He doesn't try to explain hip-hop to me. I leave it all up to him."

NU AMERICAN DREAM

These days, Simmons works hard at being a role model. As he says: "I manage people creatively, not really as a business. I tell the kids at Phat Farm to be honest, have integrity." He once asked them to read Deepak Chopra's *The Seven Spiritual Laws of Success*, and write a report. Simmons is also the cultural standard-bearer. "Everybody has to learn his philosophy," says Myorr Janha, vice president of marketing. "The Nu American Dream means to have high aspirations in life, that it's possible to be an entrepreneur. Classic American Flava means we want to be accepted by all without forgetting we're born out of hip-hop."

This, then, is the company that Russell Simmons is trying to sell to Kellwood, to Tommy Hilfiger, to the Gap, to almost anyone who can help him become what he really wants to be: an institution. "We want to sell a bunch of jeans, suits, furniture, jewelry, lingerie. Kimora is going to sell a bunch of women's clothes," he says. "We want to be distributed in Greenwich, Connecticut." This, for Simmons, is the Nu American Dream.

MONDAY MORNING...

THE PROBLEM

Maintaining company growth as hip-hop inevitably fades in popularity with the youth market

Keeping the business' cutting edge status even while partnering with decidedly unhip megacompanies

THE SOLUTION

Offer a growing diversity of products, from children's and adult clothing to athletic wear and debit cards.

Forge relationships with corporate giants that will enable the company to extend its reach.

Maintain the integrity of the brand through philanthropic and political ventures that will underscore the company's commitment to hip-hop culture.

SUSTAINING THE WIN

Continue to focus on building the business' mainstream popularity so that it will continue to thrive even when hip-hop is no longer hip.

REACHING AN AUDIENCE OF ONE: BUZZ MARKETING, THE VANISHING MASS MARKET, AND CULT BRANDS

Forget the tried-and-true marketing strategies. As mass media devolve into thousands of niche radio, Web, print, and cable players, and as skepticism about advertising increases, even the blue-chip giants are trying new marketing tactics. Some of the riskiest—buzz marketing, cult branding, and micromarketing—also offer the biggest payoffs. This chapter kicks off with the seminal article that lifted the lid on a tactic that all marketers now embrace: buzz marketing, a hot stealth strategy that is fraught with risks. It's the classic, and you read it in *BusinessWeek* first in 2001. The next section is from "The Vanishing Mass Market," an essay that deftly weaves together elements of a crucial market trend, one that touches nearly every business and will profoundly affect how products are sold and how mass media are financed. And finally, there is "Cult Brands," which laid out the new thinking that's rippling through the realm of marketing. The hottest brands are those that are creating a cultlike following among customers by interaction via the Internet and by customizing products to satisfy buyers' whims.

CREATING A BUZZ

If you frequent the right cafes in Sunset Plaza, Melrose, or the Third Street Promenade in and around Los Angeles, you're likely to encounter a gang of sleek, impossibly attractive motorbike riders who seem genuinely interested in getting to know you over an iced latte. Compliment them on their Vespa scooters glinting in the brilliant curbside sunlight, and they'll happily pull out a pad and scribble down an address and phone number—not theirs, but that of the local "boutique" where you can buy your own Vespa, just as (they'll confide) the rap artist Sisqó and the movie queen Sandra Bullock recently did.

That's when the truth hits you: this isn't a spontaneous encounter. Those scooter-riding models are on the Vespa payroll, and they've been hired to generate some favorable word of mouth for the recently reissued European bikes. The goal: to seek out trendsetters and subtly push them into talking up the brand to their friends and admirers.

Welcome to the world of buzz marketing, where brand come-ons sometimes are veiled to the point of opacity and where it is the consumers themselves who are lured into doing the heavy lifting of spreading the message. As the traditional media fragment and cynicism about advertising grows, most blue-chip marketers are trying out buzz, hoping to replicate such overnight sensations as the Harry Potter book series and Razor kick scooters. In each case, buzz that seemed to come from out of nowhere transformed what otherwise would have been a niche product into a mass phenomenon.

And that's not the only experimenting that's going on. As the expensive traditional approaches, such as network TV ads, are seemingly less able to move the needle, lots of big players are starting to push aside conventional marketing approaches and turn to hot new trends: micromarketing and cult branding.

Coca-Cola, McDonald's, General Motors, Unilever Group, American Express, and Procter & Gamble are among the many companies that are now standing mass marketing on its head by shifting their emphasis from selling to the vast, anonymous crowd to micromarketing, or selling to millions of particular consumers. The reason: the proliferation of digital and wireless communication channels is spreading the mass audience of yore ever thinner across hundreds of narrowcast cable TV and radio channels, thousands of specialized magazines, and millions of computer terminals, video-game consoles, personal digital assistants, and cell phone screens. "Every one of our brands is targeted," says James R. Stengel, P&G's global marketing officer. "You find the people. You are very focused on them. You become relevant to them."

Some of the most recognizable global brands, like Apple and Harley-Davidson, also are creating and maintaining a cultlike following among customers through the Internet and by customizing products to satisfy customers' whims. The Internet has enabled customers to gather information, talk back, and talk to one another,

which can lead to a groundswell of positive buzz for a product—
or spawn a revolt. That seismic shift in clout from companies to
customers is an opportunity for marketers that learn how to build
strong user communities. But all these new techniques also have
challenges and risks, especially for traditional brands that are
struggling to retain their leads in a market where consumers are
increasingly resisting what they see as bland ubiquity and a surfeit
of power.

THE HOT NEW STEALTH STRATEGY
Buzz marketing, with its large element of theatricality, was honed
by Hollywood studios, liquor companies, and other marketers
whose products either were outlawed in traditional media or simply
had too short a shelf life for a full-blown ad campaign. The technique
got a big theoretical lift from Malcolm Gladwell's best-selling book,
The Tipping Point: How Little Things Can Make a Big Difference, which
brought home how a small number of consumers—if they're the
right ones—can turn a grass fire into a conflagration. Now lots of
blue-chip marketers are trying to turn their
brands into carefully guarded secrets that
are revealed to a knowing few in each
community, who in turn tell a few more,
who tell a few more, and so on. Rather than
blitzing the airways with 30-second TV
commercials for its new Focus subcompact,
Ford Motor Co. recruited a handful of
trendsetters in a few markets and gave
each of them a Focus to drive for six
months. Their duties? Simply to be seen
with the car and to hand out Focus-themed
trinkets to anyone who expressed interest
in it.

At a time when young consumers are suspicious of slick advertising, buzz marketing can be a powerful sales tool, as the product endorsement seems to be coming from a cool friend rather than from an anonymous corporate conglomerate.

Often buzz marketers try to cover their tracks, at least initially,
as Vespa is doing with its biker impersonators. Other times, though,
it's immediately clear who the sponsor is, as when Lucky Strike sent
teams to bring iced coffee and beach chairs to exiled smokers
trying to catch a smoke outside urban office buildings. Either way,
the gambit essentially is the same: to slip into the conversational
pathways of those who heavily influence their peers. That way,

instead of coming from a faceless and distrusted corporate conglomerate, the marketing message seems to emanate from the most powerful endorser possible: your coolest friend.

But measuring the reach of a buzz campaign has nowhere near the precision of AC Nielsen Corp. ratings or cost-per-thousand magazine subscribers. And while buzz may work for products with a heavy dose of fashion, there's skepticism that it will translate to more prosaic categories, such as paper towels and breakfast cereal. There is also the risk that buzz will simply be overdone and will lose its power to capture attention by becoming too familiar—or may even provoke a backlash. "Our clients have to know that if you are trying to be subversive and you are found out, it can be dangerous," says Scott Leonard, CEO of ADD Marketing Inc., an agency that uses street teams and chat-room "cyber-reps" to spread hot, not-always-flattering gossip about client company recording artists.

Staid IBM ran afoul of the law back in 2001 when one of its agencies stenciled wordless images of a peace symbol, a heart, and a penguin on Chicago and San Francisco sidewalks to build buzz for its "Peace Love Linux" effort behind the open-source software. True, the resulting avalanche of media coverage did more than expensive paid ads could have done to draw attention to IBM's Linux effort, but Big Blue's portrayal as a corporate vandal may not have been the image it was looking for.

In fact, the growing popularity of buzz marketing could well spell its downfall. After all, buzz is inherently exclusive, not inclusive. Once everyone does it, it's no longer buzz; it's simply obscure—and annoying—advertising. "The biggest problem with buzz marketing . . . will be the glut of people trying to do it," says Jonathan Ressler, CEO of Big Fat Promotions, which worked on the Lucky Strike effort. By then, marketers that are looking to break free from the herd will have to resort to something more unusual. Super Bowl ads, anyone?

> The catch: buzz may not work for ordinary products, like toilet paper, and overuse could cause a consumer backlash.

THE VANISHING MASS MARKET

Last year, Americans bought some $2 billion worth of Tide, which has ranked as the country's biggest-selling laundry detergent ever since Procter & Gamble Co. took it national in 1949. If ever a brand epitomized the great, one-size-fits-all mass market, it is Tide, right? Wrong. Or so says P&G. James Stengel, P&G's global marketing officer, insists that his company's bulging portfolio of big brands contains "not one mass-market brand, whether it's Tide or Old Spice"— or Crest or Pampers or Ivory.

Likewise, McDonald's has devoted a third of its U.S. marketing budget to television, compared with two-thirds more than five years ago. Money that used to go for 30-second network spots now pays for closed-circuit sports programming piped into Hispanic bars and for ads in *Upscale*, a custom-published magazine distributed to black barbershops. To sharpen its appeal to young men, McDonald's even advertises on Foot Locker Inc.'s in-store video network. "We are a big marketer," says M. Lawrence Light, McDonald's chief marketing officer, echoing Stengel's disavowals. "We are not a mass marketer."

For marketers, the evolution from mass marketing to micromarketing is a fundamental change, driven as much by necessity as by opportunity. America has atomized into countless market segments, defined not only by demography, but by increasingly nuanced and insistent product preferences. "All the research we're doing tells us that the driver of demand going forward is all about products that are 'right for me,'" says David Martin, president of Interbrand Corp. "And that's ultimately about offering a degree of customization for all."

At the same time, the almost-universal audience assembled long ago by network television is eroding. In the 1960s, an advertiser could reach 80 percent of U.S. women with a spot aired simultaneously on CBS, NBC, and ABC. Today, an ad would have to run on 100 TV channels to have a prayer of duplicating this feat. Adding a few Web sites would help, but not even the biggest new media conduits—not Home Box Office, not Yahoo! not AOL Instant Messenger, not even X-Box—is likely to ever match the ubiquity of the Big Three networks in their prime.

On balance, the dawning era of micromarketing holds great promise for consumer marketers and, by extension, for the U.S. economy. By adding hugely to the overall supply of advertising time and space, the proliferation of new communications can be expected to tamp down ad-rate inflation. Targeting might also be a boon to corporate productivity, as companies are spending the same money but getting a bigger boost.

At the same time, though, the fading of the age of mass marketing poses a threat to the traditional mass media and their heavily ad-dependent business models. There is not much that broadcast TV, the quintessential mass medium, can do to accommodate the growing demand for targeting. Cable continues to nibble away at its broadcast rivals by adding highly specialized channels and such services as video-on-demand. Print, the oldest mass medium, has been "niching down" for decades but appears to be bumping up against the limits of its adaptability—at least when it comes to creating themed newspaper sections or demographically targeted editions of magazines.

The Internet is rapidly coming of age as an advertising medium, with the crude banner and pop-up ads that initially defined online advertising giving way to larger and more refined formats. Blue-chip companies like General Motors Corp. and SBC Communications are becoming among the largest Internet advertisers, as digital media offer two distinct advantages. First, they enable marketers to gather reams of invaluable personal information directly from customers and adjust their sales pitch accordingly, in some cases in real time. Second, they permit a fuller and more precise measuring of advertising's impact. "Advertisers want to exactly know what they are paying for and what they are getting for it, and you really get metrics on the Web," says David Verklin, CEO of Carat North America, a media-buying agency.

Micromarketing—selling to different consumer segments rather than the masses—is not merely a response to the fragmenting of the mass media. It's an attempt by marketers to address consumer demand for customized products.

The rise of micromarketing is as much a response to the fragmentation of consumer markets as it is to the fragmentation of the mass audience. In the 1950s and 1960s, the country was far more uniform in terms not only of ethnicity—the great Hispanic influx had not yet begun—but also of aspiration. The governing ideal was not merely to keep up with the Joneses, but to be the Joneses—to own the same model of car or dishwasher or lawn mower. As levels of affluence rose markedly in the 1970s and 1980s, status was redefined. "From the

consumer point of view," says McDonald's
Light, "we've had a change from 'I want to
be normal' to 'I want to be special.'"

As companies competed to indulge this
yearning, they began to elaborate mass
production into mass customization. As a
walk down any supermarket aisle makes
plain, the consumer is awash in choice, but
that has made it harder to attract buyers in
a clamorous marketplace surfeited with
virtually identical products and marketing

Staying on message is
not easy in digital
media, as the Internet
has shifted the power
from companies
to consumers,
empowering
customers to mobilize
public opinion for,
and against, products.

come-ons. So not only are packaged-goods companies becoming
more selective in their use of mass advertising, but they're also
starting to gather personal information about consumers' attitudes,
desires, and habits. It's all about "relevance," the micromarketer's
mantra.

American shoppers are studied in their homes by teams of
cultural anthropologists and are pursued over the telephone and
online by survey takers of all sorts. Over the past few years, Grey
Worldwide has conducted more than 100,000 interviews and has
spent millions of dollars to devise a methodology for identifying the
particular emotions that lead people to buy particular products. It
might sound like mumbo jumbo, but believers include P&G's Stengel.
"The future of marketing will be much more oriented to permission
marketing—marketing plans and advertising so relevant that it is
welcomed by consumers," Stengel says.

The progress of micromarketing appears to be inexorable,
favored as it is by both economics and demographics. Certainly there
is no stopping media proliferation, for it is providing consumers with
what they crave: a wealth of new content and innovative modes of
consuming it. The mass market will not disappear, nor will the mass
media. But the fortunes of many of America's best-known companies
now will rise or fall depending on how well they adapt to what is
shaping up to be a long and chaotic transition from the fading age
of mass marketing to the dawning era of micromarketing.

THE NEW CULT BRANDS

Casey Neistat, 23, is a self-professed Apple junkie. Along with his
brother, Van, he is building his filmmaking career with the company's

iMac computers and editing software. He usually leaves his Manhattan apartment with a sleek iPod plugged into his ear. So when the Neistat brothers discovered that the digital music player's batteries were irreplaceable and lasted just 18 months, they made a film called *iPod's Dirty Secret* and launched a protest Web site. Apple Computer Inc. addressed the problem. Now Neistat insists that the protest was an act of love: "We made that film because we believe in the brand so much."

Such loyalty flies in the face of conventional marketing wisdom. A customer spurned, the logic goes, is a customer lost. But these days, consumers are demanding more from the brands they love than simple reliability. Increasingly, consumers are customizing products and services as a means of self-expression—whether it's tailoring the colors on a pair of sneakers from Nike Inc. or adding items to their personal to-watch list on eBay. No longer passively consuming, they're beginning to act and feel like owners or members of a community. As Peter Weedfald, senior vice president for strategic marketing and new media at Samsung Electronics North America, puts it: "Consumers are empowered in a way that's almost frightening."

There have always been cult brands, mostly smaller labels that are unknown to the masses. But these days, building cults, or at least strong communities, is a widespread strategy. No wonder companies that are able to instill a sense of ownership in near-fanatical customers showed the biggest gains in our fourth annual ranking of the 100 most valuable global brands. The loyal, if sometimes nagging, band of true believers behind number 43, Apple—combined with the tremendous success of the iPod—helped the dollar value of the brand jump 23.7 percent, to $6.9 billion in 2005. That was the biggest increase in this year's ranking, which is compiled in partnership with leading brand consultancy Interbrand Corp. A dollar value is calculated for each brand using a mix of publicly available data, projected profits, and variables like market leadership. Meanwhile, behemoths like the $67.4 billion Coca-Cola brand or the $61.4 billion Microsoft are starting to recognize the need to nurture stronger ties with consumers. Witness moves by Microsoft to hold mini trade shows in airport lounges for consumers and the soda giant's creation of hip "Coke Red Lounges" for teens in suburban malls.

The brands that have managed to build cultlike followings have done so by having clearly defined and rigorously enforced values. And the fastest-growing ones often project an aura, an attractive group identity. Conjure up an image of an Armani customer or a Porsche driver and it will evoke a set of personality characteristics as much as it evokes a product preference. They also beget proselytizers—customers who will chat up the brands to their buddies, set up Web sites, attend events, and proudly identify themselves as adherents, according to strategist Douglas Atkin of ad agency Merkley & Partners, who recently wrote *The Culting of Brands* (Portfolio Hardcover, 2004). Nobody has to pay them. They are owners as well as customers.

The classic example of a cult brand is Harley-Davidson. The 101-year-old brand gained 4 percent in value in 2004, to $7.1 billion. Sure, there are new models like the sleek V-Rod line and fresh features aimed at wooing women, but the real buzz comes from the 886,000 members of the company-sponsored Harley Owners Group. They're the ones who organize rides, training courses, social events, and charity fund raisers.

The key for brand builders is to give empowered consumers a great product and the tools to use it however they want. For Jeffrey P. Bezos, chief executive of Amazon.com, whose brand value grew 22 percent, that means allowing negative customer reviews, even if it sabotages a possible sale. Some companies allow customers to set up fan sites on the Web or personalize items. Numbers 18, Honda Motor and Nike, offer tools to help customers put their imprint on a product—such as choosing unique color combinations and messages for their sneakers.

In contrast, some old-line brands seem to be coasting on sheer size rather than their ability to forge a unique relationship with their customers. Over the past year, heavyweights like Microsoft, Coca-Cola, and Walt Disney saw their brand values erode.

POWER PLAY

The hottest brands today are those that create a cultlike following among customers by being self-consciously different from their rivals and developing strong user communities. That can mean permitting customers to set up fan sites on the Web— or allowing them to pan a product on the company's own Web site, as Amazon does.

Others, like Finnish mobile-phone giant Nokia Corp., number 8, are struggling to regain momentum.

That doesn't mean that big brands can't connect with customers. Even massive players like General Electric Co., number 4, which saw its brand value gain 4 percent, to $44.1 billion, can adopt a fun, flirty style. The most popular section on the company's Web site is the "GE Pen," which allows users to doodle in a variety of colors and styles before e-mailing their handiwork to a friend. Within one year of launching, it had received more than 43 million impressions.

Does this help the company sell more ovens or more advertising on NBC? Probably not. But it certainly gives users a warmer feeling about GE. These days, anything that makes fans out of fickle consumers can be priceless in building a brand.

Trends is drawn from Gerry Khermouch with Jeff Green, "Buzz Marketing," July 30, 2001; Anthony Bianco with Tom Lowry, Robert Berner, Ronald Grover, "The Vanishing Mass Market," July 12, 2004; and Diane Brady with Robert D. Hof, Andy Reinhardt, Moon Ihlwan, Stanley Holmes, Kerry Capell, "Cult Brands," August 2, 2004.

SOURCES

Chapter 1: Tom Lowry, with Mark Hyman, Ronald Grover, and Roger Crockett, "ESPN: The Empire," October 17, 2005; http://www.businessweek.com/magazine/content/05_42/b3955001.htm.

Chapter 2: Michael Arndt, "Cat Sinks Its Claws into Services," December 5, 2005; http://www.businessweek.com/magazine/content/05_49/b3962096.htm.

Chapter 3: Mara Der Hovanesian, "Thinking Locally at Citigroup," October 24, 2005; http://www.businessweek.com/magazine/content/05_43/b3956119.htm.

Chapter 4: Cliff Edwards, "Intel Inside Out," January 9, 2006; http://www.businessweek.com/magazine/content/06_02/b3966001.htm.

Chapter 5: Ariane Sains and Stanley Reed, with Michael Arndt, "Electrolux Cleans Up," February 26, 2006; http://www.businessweek.com/magazine/content/06_09/b3973071.htm.

Chapter 6: Jack Ewing with Andrea Zammert, Wendy Zellner, Rachel Tiplady, Ellen Groves, and Michael Eidam, "The Next Wal-Mart?" April 26, 2004; http://www.businessweek.com/magazine/content/04_17/b3880010.htm. Larry Armstrong, "Trader Joe's: The Trendy American Cousin," April 26, 2004; http://www.businessweek.com/magazine/content/04_17/b3880016.htm.

Chapter 7: Peter Burrows, "HP's Ultimate Team Player," January 30, 2006; http://www.businessweek.com/magazine/content/06_05/b3969071.htm.

Chapter 8: Amy Barrett, "J&J: Reinventing How It Invents," April 17, 2006; http://www.businessweek.com/magazine/content/06_16/b3980081.htm.

Chapter 9:   Tom Lowry, "Can MTV Stay Cool?" February 20, 2006; http://www.businessweek.com/magazine/content/06_08/b3972001.htm.

Chapter 10: Kerry Capell, with Ariane Sains, Cristina Lindblad, Ann Therese Palmer, Jason Bush, Dexter Roberts, and Kenji Hall, "Ikea: How the Swedish Retailer Became a Global Cult Brand," November 14, 2005; http://www.business week.com/magazine/content/05_46/b3959001.htm.

Chapter 11: Diane Brady, "The Education of Jeff Immelt," April 29, 2002; http://www.businessweek.com/magazine/content/02_17/b3780001.htm.

Chapter 12: Ben Elgin, "Managing Google's Idea Factory," October 3, 2005; http://www.businessweek.com/magazine/content/05_40/b3953093.htm.

Chapter 13: Peter Burrows and Ronald Grover, with Heather Green, "Steve Jobs' Magic Kingdom," February 6, 2006; http://www.businessweek.com/magazine/content/06_06/b3970001.htm.

Chapter 14: Michael Arndt with Diane Brady, "3M's Rising Star," April 12, 2004; http://www.businessweek.com/magazine/content/04_15/b3878001_mz001.htm.

Chapter 15: Susan Berfield with Diane Brady and Tom Lowry, "The CEO of Hip-Hop," October 27, 2003; http://www.businessweek.com/magazine/content/03_43/b3855001_mz001.htm.

TRENDS: Gerry Khermouch with Jeff Green, "Buzz Marketing," July 30, 2001; http://www.businessweek.com/magazine/content/01_31/b3743001.htm; Anthony Bianco with Tom Lowry, Robert Berner, Ronald Grover, "The Vanishing Mass Market," July 12, 2004; http://www.businessweek.com/magazine/content/04_28/b3891001_mz001.htm?chan=search; Diane Brady with Robert D. Hof, Andy Reinhardt, Moon Ihlwan, Stanley Holmes, Kerry Capell, "Cult Brands," August 2, 2004; http://www.businessweek.com/magazine/content/04_31/b3894094.htm?chan=search.

CONTRIBUTORS

TOM LOWRY is a senior writer for *BusinessWeek*, responsible for the magazine's media and entertainment coverage. Prior to this position, Mr. Lowry was media editor for the magazine. He has penned and/or edited six cover stories since 2004, including "Can MTV Stay Cool?," a profile of CEO Judy McGrath and her efforts to remake her company for a digital world: "ESPN, The Empire," an analysis of how the hottest brand in sports plans to stay on top of rivals, and "Rupert's World," one of the first articles to add up all the Aussie mogul's vast and growing powers. Another cover, "MegaMerger," was completed in one day after Comcast made a hostile bid for Disney. "Nascar" ran the same week as the Comcast story as a regional cover on Southern newsstands, making Lowry the only *BusinessWeek*-er ever to have two covers in one week. He also wrote "Yao!," a sports biz story on the Chinese basketball phenom.

Other cover story subjects have included the Vanishing Mass Market, Dick Parsons, Comcast, the NFL, and Bloomberg LP.

Lowry, an alumnus of the University of Delaware, was a Knight-Bagehot Fellow in Business and Economics Journalism at the Columbia Graduate School of Journalism. A newspaper veteran, he also did stints at the *New York Daily News* and *USA Today,* among others, before coming to *BusinessWeek* in 1999.

MARK HYMAN is a contributing editor at *BusinessWeek*. He is responsible for covering the sports business section as well as consulting on any stories that deal with sports and sports business.

During his 20 years as a journalist, Mr. Hyman has worked for five newspapers, including the *Baltimore Sun,* where he was part of investigative teams nominated for Pulitzer prizes.

In 1998 Simon and Schuster published *Confessions of a Baseball Pursuit,* a book on which Mr. Hyman collaborated with broadcaster Jon Miller.

Mr. Hyman won second place for the Associated Press Sports Editors Award "Best Investigative Story" in 1983, on a report he wrote about the NCAA rule violations. He also received third place for the 1992 APSE Award "Best News Story," with a story on the bankruptcy filing of the Baltimore Orioles owner.

Mr. Hyman received a bachelor's degree from the University of Pennsylvania and degree in law from the University of Maryland.

RONALD GROVER is Los Angeles bureau manager for *BusinessWeek,* a position he assumed in 1987. He has written numerous cover stories, including "The Future of California" (April 30, 2001) and "Hollywood Heist" (July 14, 2003), as well as articles on Disney, Michael Ovitz, Steven Spielberg, and the media and entertainment industry. Mr. Grover is also the author of the 1991 book, *The Disney Touch* (2ed., McGraw-Hill, 1996).

Mr. Grover joined The McGraw-Hill Companies, the parent company of *BusinessWeek,* in 1975 as a reporter for McGraw-Hill energy newsletter in Washington, D.C. In 1979, be became energy correspondent for McGraw-Hill World News in Washington, D.C. From 1982 to 1986 he was *BusinessWeek*'s congressional correspondent, covering economic and political issues, including tax reform, fiscal policy, and trade legislation. He moved to *BusinessWeek*'s Los Angeles bureau in 1986 as a correspondent, covering entertainment, politics, and other business news, which he continues to cover in his present post. Prior to joining McGraw-Hill, Mr. Grover was a reporter for *The Washington Star.*

Mr. Grover has appeared on numerous national television and radio programs including CNBC's *Kudlow and Cramer, America Now,* and *Squawk Box,* as well as PBS's *The News Hour with Jim Lehrer.* Most recently, he appeared on CNBC's *Kudlow and Cramer,* discussing the "Hollywood Heist" cover story.

Mr. Grover holds a bachelor's degree in political science and a master's in business administration from George Washington University and a master's degree from the Columbia University Graduate School of Journalism.

ROGER CROCKETT is the Chicago Deputy Bureau Manager for *BusinessWeek*, a position he assumed in 2006. He is responsible for covering telecommunications and technology, the Internet and e-commerce, and race and cultural issues in business. Previously, he was a Chicago correspondent for *BusinessWeek*.

Prior to joining *BusinessWeek*, Mr. Crockett was the technology and telecommunications reporter for *The (Portland) Oregonian,* covered the cereal industry for the *Battle Creek Enquirer* in Michigan, and was a reporter/researcher at *Newsweek* in New York.

Mr. Crockett holds a bachelor's degree in English from UCLA and a master's in journalism from the Columbia Graduate School of Journalism.

MICHAEL ARNDT is a senior correspondent in the *BusinessWeek* Chicago Bureau. He is responsible for covering airlines, basic manufacturing, health care, and commercial real estate.

Prior to joining *BusinessWeek*, Mr. Arndt was the Sunday business editor for the *Chicago Tribune* for two years. Before that, Mr. Arndt was the *Chicago Tribune*'s acting financial editor, chief economics correspondent in Washington, D.C., and a business reporter coverimg several countries in Europe.

In 2000, Mr. Arndt was nominated for the Peter Ligasor award from the Chicago Headline Club for a story on United Airlines. His "Management Lessons from the Bust" article made him a joint winner of the same award in 2001. During the same year, Mr. Arndt made an appearance on the ABC *Evening News with Peter Jennings*. A successful year in 2001 was followed by his appearance with the PBS CEO Exchange in 2002.

Mr. Arndt started his career in 1980 at the City News Bureau and is a graduate of the University of Wisconsin.

MARA DER HOVANESIAN is the Finance and Banking department editor at *BusinessWeek*. Before joining *BusinessWeek* in May 2000, she covered the mutual fund and personal finance industries for Dow Jones & Co. and Knight-Ridder newspapers. Her work has appeared in the *Wall Street Journal* and other major metropolitan newspapers nationwide.

Ms. Der Hovanesian received her master's degree in economics from California State University in San Francisco in 1990. She won a first place award from the Associated Press for business writing in

1996 and a scholarship to the Institute for Political Journalism at Georgetown University in 1986.

CLIFF EDWARDS is a correspondent in *BusinessWeek*'s San Mateo bureau, where he covers Intel, the semiconductor industry, handheld- and consumer-electronics companies.

Prior to joining *BusinessWeek*, Mr. Edwards worked for The Associated Press. During a 12-year span at the Associated Press, Mr. Edwards held several positions. He most recently covered technology issues and companies. He also served as business editor, overseeing six Illinois-based correspondents and handling stories that ranged from UAL Corp.'s employee buyout to a price-fixing scandal at Archer Daniels Midland Co. Before that, he broke news on Chicago's killer heat wave and covered presidential elections and the Democratic National Convention in Chicago.

Mr. Edwards received both his bachelor's and master's degrees from Northwestern University, where he was also an adjunct professor of journalism for seven years. He was a finalist in Chicago's Charlie Chamberlain awards for wire service coverage.

STANLEY REED has been London Bureau Chief of *BusinessWeek* since August 1996. He took on the additional role of Middle East correspondent in 1999. Prior to coming to London he held a series of editing positions at *BusinessWeek* in New York.

In London his beat includes finance, the international oil industry, Scandinavia, and British politics and economic policy. Mr. Reed lived in Cairo from 1976-1980 and has written for such publications as *The New York Times, Foreign Affairs,* and *Foreign Policy* as well as for *BusinessWeek*.

Mr. Reed is a graduate of Yale University and Columbia Business School. He was a Knight-Bagehot Fellow at Columbia University Journalism School in 1987-1988. He was president of the Association of American Correspondents in London for 1998 and remains a member of the organization's executive board.

JACK EWING is the Frankfurt bureau chief for *BusinessWeek*, a position he assumed in August 1999. He is responsible for leading German and Central Europe coverage for the magazine.

As Bureau chief, Mr. Ewing has covered stories that include a narrative about the fall of German media czar Leo Kirch (March 11, 2002) and a portrait of former Bertelsmann CEO Thomas Middelhoff (November 13, 2000). Prior to becoming bureau chief, Mr. Ewing was a Frankfurt correspondent, covering stories that ranged from corporate raiders to telecom reform. Mr. Ewing has made numerous appearances on television and radio, including BBC-TV, BBC Radio, Deutsche Welle TV, and German Public Television.

Mr. Ewing joined *BusinessWeek* from Bloomberg News, where he was a deputy bureau chief in Frankfurt and editor responsible for coverage on the economics of the euro zone. Before moving to Germany in 1994, Mr. Ewing was a political and legal reporter for *The Hartford Courant*. He has written for the *Christian Science Monitor, The Wall Street Journal Europe, The Independent, Variety*, and the Associated Press. He has also appeared as a commentator on the McLaughlin Group, BBC World, Deutsche Welle, and Hessische Rundfunk radio.

Mr. Ewing is a graduate of Hampshire College in Amherst, Massachusetts, and holds a master's degree in history from Trinity College in Hartford, Connecticut. Mr. Ewing is a German Marshall Fund European Union Fellow.

WENDY ZELLNER was *BusinessWeek*'s Dallas bureau manager, and covered the airline industry, along with a variety of other major companies in the bureau's territory, comprising Texas, Arkansas, Louisiana, and Oklahoma.

PETER BURROWS is the department editor of *BusinessWeek*'s West Coast computer coverage. Based in San Mateo, he oversees the magazine's coverage of the hardware world, from PCs and handheld devices to mainframes and back-office storage gear. He also covers some of the key West Coast computer companies, including Cisco Systems, Apple, and Pixar Animation.

Prior to this position, he was a senior correspondent in the San Mateo bureau. Mr. Burrows joined *BusinessWeek* in 1993 as a Dallas correspondent, responsible for covering the computer, semiconductor and energy industries. Prior to joining *BusinessWeek*, he was a senior editor for *Electronic Business* magazine.

Over the years, Mr. Burrows has chronicled the ups and downs of some of Silicon Valley's top stories: the fall and rise of Apple under Steve Jobs, Sun Microsystems CEO Scott McNealy's crusade against Microsoft, and the controversial tenure of Carly Fiorina at Hewlett-Packard. He is also the author of *Backfire: Carly Fiorina's High-Stakes Battle for the Soul of Hewlett-Packard* (Wiley, 2003). Mr. Burrows has appeared on CNBC, PBS, and CNNfn, as well as various radio stations.

Mr. Burrows holds a bachelor's degree in political science from Colgate University and a master's in journalism from Columbia University Graduate School of Journalism.

AMY BARRETT is the Philadelphia Bureau Chief for *BusinessWeek*, a position she assumed in 1998.

Prior to that, Ms. Barrett was the Philadelphia correspondent, covering the pharmaceutical industry, and regional business from New Jersey to Baltimore. She assumed this position in July 1997. Ms. Barrett joined *BusinessWeek* in 1992 as Los Angeles correspondent and in 1994 became the Washington, D.C. correspondent. She was responsible for covering banking and corporate finance.

Ms. Barrett came to *BusinessWeek* from *Financial World* magazine, where she began as a writer and was later named bureau chief. Prior to that, she was a credit analyst for Thompson McKinnon.

Ms. Barrett holds a bachelor's degree in finance from the University of Pennsylvania Wharton School of Business.

KERRY CAPELL is a London Correspondent at *BusinessWeek*, a position she assumed in January 1999. Ms. Capell is responsible for covering the European pharmaceutical and biotech industries. She also handles all of the magazine's coverage of Ireland, focusing on economic, political and corporate news and analysis. Ms. Capell also regularly writes on Britain's telecom, media, and aviation industries. Prior to joining the London Bureau, she was the international finance editor for *BusinessWeek*, a position she assumed in July 1997. Since September 1995, she has been a staff editor in the personal business section, covering personal finance and investing.

Ms. Capell joined *BusinessWeek* from *Financial Planning* magazine, where she was managing editor. Ms. Capell holds a bachelor's degree in political science from Catholic University and a master's degree in international affairs from Columbia University.

CRISTINA LINDBLAD is Europe editor for *BusinessWeek*, a position she assumed in December 2001. She is responsible for all European coverage for both domestic and international editions of the magazine. Prior to this position, Ms. Lindblad was Latin America editor and also developed coverage of the region for *BusinessWeek Online.*

Prior to joining *BusinessWeek*, Ms. Lindblad was the editor for the Economist Intelligence Unit's weekly publication, *Business Latin America.* She has written extensively on Latin issues as a correspondent and associate editor and has worked closely with writers in the region. Prior to that, she worked for CBS reports and the Associated Press.

Ms. Lindblad received a bachelor's degree from Barnard College and a master's degree in international affairs from Columbia University.

ANN THERESE PALMER started working as a freelance reporter for *BusinessWeek* in 1976, while she was attending law school at Loyola University, Chicago. After passing the bar, she was a tax attorney at Esmark, Inc., a Chicago conglomerate that included Swift Meat and Playtex. Subsequently, she became general counsel for Chicago United, an urban affairs coalition of CEOs.

She returned to *BusinessWeek* as a freelancer in 1990. She covers stories relating to financial, corporate, and education issues. In addition, she is currently a special correspondent for the *Chicago Tribune* business section and writes for the University of Notre Dame Mendoza College of Business magazine. A Detroit native, she's a "Double Domer" (Notre Dame graduate), a member of the first class of women undergraduates and a recipient of a master's of business administration from that university.

JASON BUSH is the bureau chief of *BusinessWeek*'s Moscow bureau. He is responsible for coverage of business and politics in Russia and the former Soviet Union. Previously, he was a correspondent in Moscow, a position he assumed in 2003.

Prior to joining *BusinessWeek,* Mr. Bush was a freelance business journalist in Moscow for several years. He contributed pieces to the *Economist Intelligence Unit, BusinessWeek, Institutional Investor, Emerging Markets,* and *Business Eastern Europe.* Before that, he was a staff writer at *Business Central Europe* magazine and *Central European* magazine.

Mr. Bush holds a bachelor's degree in philosophy, politics, and economics from Corpus Christi College and a master's in history from Tufts University.

DEXTER T. ROBERTS is the Bureau Manager Beijing for *BusinessWeek.*

As a freelance writer, he has written for such publications as the *New Asia Review, Asian Wall Street Journal, Associated Press,* and *Agence France-Presse.* He has also held positions as research director for the Taiwan International Conference, curriculum coordinator and English teacher for the National Taiwan University, and as guest lecturer with the Mongolia National University, School of Foreign Service.

Mr. Roberts holds a bachelor's degree in political science from Stanford University and a master's in international affairs from Columbia University's School of International and Public Affairs.

KENJI HALL is a correspondent based in *BusinessWeek*'s Tokyo bureau, covering technology and science. He has reported from Japan for eight years.

Before joining *BusinessWeek* in August 2005, Mr. Hall spent nearly five years at the Associated Press, where he wrote about economics, science and natural disasters from Japan and other parts of Asia.

Mr. Hall received his bachelor's from Harvard University in 1993 and is a native of San Diego, California.

DIANE BRADY is a senior writer, covering corporations for *BusinessWeek.* She is responsible for coverage of New York area companies, such as General Electric and Martha Stewart Living Omnimedia, and such areas as marketing, corporate trends, and workplace issues. Previously, Ms. Brady was an associate editor in the corporations department and Connecticut bureau chief at *BusinessWeek*, a position she assumed January 1, 1999. Along with covering the key companies in Connecticut, she was also in charge of coverage for much of New Jersey and greater New York.

Ms. Brady's most recent cover stories include "The Unsung CEO," about United Technology's George David, "Act Two," which takes a look at Ann Fudge's return to work life after two years, and "The Education of Jeff Immelt," about Jack Welch's replacement at GE. Ms. Brady has made numerous appearances on television and radio, including CNN's *People in the News,* NBC's *Dateline*, A&E's *Biography*, as well as various CNBC, NY-1, CNNfn, and MSNBC programs. She has also guest-hosted *MoneyTalk with Bob Brinker* on ABC's radio network. Additionally, she is a regular guest on ABC's *World News This Morning* and Canada's CBC and ROB-TV networks.

Prior to joining *BusinessWeek*, Ms. Brady was with *Asian Wall Street Journal,* where she was a staff reporter in Hong Kong and other parts of the region for four years. Before that, she was an associate editor at *Maclean's Magazine* in Toronto. She was also a speechwriter for the UN Environment Programme in Nairobi, Kenya.

Ms. Brady has received numerous awards and honors, including two National Magazine Awards in Canada, the Deadline Club Award for Best Business Reporting, the Front Page Award from the Newswoman's Club of New York, and the Journalist of the Year Award from Pacific Asia Travel Association. She also received a McGraw-Hill Corporate Achievement Award for Editorial Excellence, and was a finalist for the Henry Chapin Media Award.

BEN ELGIN is a correspondent for *BusinessWeek* in the San Mateo bureau, a position he assumed in September 2000. Mr. Elgin covers Internet companies, with a specific focus on Internet content, Net advertising, B2B exchanges, and Internet outsourcing.

Before joining *BusinessWeek*, Mr. Elgin was a senior editor and features editor at *Sm@rt Reseller* magazine from December 1997 through September 2000. He was also an associate editor for *ZDNet* from August 1996 through December 1997.

Mr. Elgin received his bachelor's in 1995 from the University of California, San Diego with a major. in communications and a minor in history.

HEATHER GREEN is the Internet editor for *BusinessWeek*'s information technology section. She is currently responsible for coverage of digital media and wireless. She writes and edits stories on online publishing and entertainment, wireless data services, and innovative Web use within companies.

Ms. Green started at *BusinessWeek* in 1997, breaking ground on a series of Internet trends in advertising, e-commerce, privacy, and digital media. As an editor, Ms. Green has handled *BusinessWeek*'s annual IT 100 list and edited covers on Web Smart corporations, digital medicine, and Internet productivity.

Prior to joining *BusinessWeek*, Ms. Green worked for three years at Bloomberg News, building from scratch the wire service's Internet beat. She was also an editorial assistant at the *International Herald Tribune* in Paris.

Ms. Green holds a graduate degree in political science and economics from the Institut d'Etudes Politiques de Paris and an undergraduate degree in comparative literature from the University of Virginia. She has won several awards, including the New York Press Club Crystal Gavel Award and the Front Page Award from the Newswomen's Club of New York.

Take your
game to the
next level
with the
BusinessWeek
Power Plays
Series.

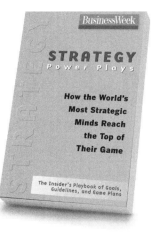

Powerful Insight for Powerful Players